TWAYNE'S WORLD AUTHORS SERIES

A Survey of the World's Literature

POLAND

Irene Nagurski

EDITOR

Contemporary Polish Poetry
1925–1975

TWAS 586

CONTEMPORARY POLISH POETRY
1925 – 1975

By MADELINE G. LEVINE

University of North Carolina

TWAYNE PUBLISHERS
A DIVISION OF G. K. HALL & CO., BOSTON

Copyright © 1981 by G. K. Hall & Co.

Published in 1981 by Twayne Publishers,
A Division of G. K. Hall & Co.
All Rights Reserved

Printed on permanent/durable acid-free paper and bound
in the United States of America

First Printing

Library of Congress Cataloging in Publication Data

Levine, Madeline G
Contemporary Polish poetry, 1925–1975.

(Twayne's world authors series ; TWAS 586 : Poland)
Bibliography: p.
Includes index.
1. Polish poetry—20th century—History and criticism.
I. Title.
PG7070.L4   891.8'57'09   81–429
ISBN 0–8057–6428–3   AACR1

For Wiktor Weintraub

Contents

About the Author

Preface

Acknowledgments

Chronology

About the Author

Madeline G. Levine is Professor of Slavic Literature and Chairman of the Department of Slavic Languages at the University of North Carolina at Chapel Hill where she teaches Polish and Russian literature. She previously taught in the Program in Comparative Literature at the Graduate School of the City University of New York. She received her B.A. from Brandeis University and her M.A. and Ph.D. degrees from Harvard University, and has done postdoctoral research at the Jagiellonian University in Cracow, Poland.

Her previously published works include articles on Polish poetry in *The Polish Review, The Slavic and East European Journal,* and Polish periodicals. She has also published an annotated translation from the Polish of Miron Białoszewski's *A Memoir of the Warsaw Uprising* (Ann Arbor: Ardis, 1977).

Preface

Contemporary Polish poetry has both a national and an international significance. Poland is a small country and the Polish language is understood by relatively few readers outside its borders, but Polish poetry of the last half century has confronted issues, both aesthetic and moral, which are central to the twentieth century. The major convulsions of recent history have engulfed the Polish nation, and the response of Polish poets is of interest to anyone who values poetry as a living art.

The value of contemporary Polish poetry is not limited to its central concerns. Among poets writing in Polish today at least three—Czesław Miłosz, Zbigniew Herbert, and Tadeusz Różewicz—are major talents who have already achieved an international reputation. All three have been ably translated into English (see the bibliography below).

The present study is intended to introduce contemporary Polish poetry in greater depth than is presently available in English, and to provide a context for understanding those Polish poets who are already familiar in English translation. It should be of interest to two classes of readers—those who know no Polish but wish to be introduced to Polish poetry, and those who have a general knowledge of Polish literature and a particular interest in the contemporary period. For this reason, all poetic examples are provided in Polish and in English translation. Unless otherwise indicated in the notes, the translations are mine.

This study aims at being representative rather than inclusive. Some of my choices may be controversial. Some readers may wonder why I have not considered here such important figures as Konstanty Ildefons Gałczyński, Władysław Broniewski, Tymoteusz Karpowicz, Jarosław Marek Rymkiewicz, or Wiktor Woroszylski, to name just a few excluded poets. The choice of representative figures is inevitably a composite of objective and subjective assessments. The representativeness of each of the ten poets studied here is outlined briefly in chapter 1. Each poet is discussed in depth in succeeding chapters. I offer this book as one portrait of the face of contemporary Polish poetry.

MADELINE G. LEVINE

University of North Carolina at Chapel Hill

Acknowledgments

In the years since I first took up the study of Polish literature at Harvard University, Professor Wiktor Weintraub has been a never failing source of inspiration, encouragement, and wise counsel. I owe him far more than a few words of thanks for reading my book in manuscript. In dedicating this book to him I hope in some small measure to acknowledge my debt to him as teacher, scholar, friend.

In writing this study I was fortunate to have two other attentive readers. Steven I. Levine, my husband and sternest critic, combed the text for bad logic and clumsy phrases. Paul Debreczeny, my colleague at the University of North Carolina at Chapel Hill, thoroughly probed each chapter with rare patience. His valuable comments filtered out many a dubious interpretation.

Magnus Jan Krynski of Duke University graciously read and commented on chapter 6. Irene Nagurski has been a considerate and helpful editor for whose tact and patience I am grateful. Robert H. Burger of the University of Illinois at Urbana provided meticulous research assistance at the outset of the project and compiled the index to the book. His work, as well as other expenses, was supported by a grant from the University Research Council of the University of North Carolina at Chapel Hill. Carolyn McDade, Elizabeth Koniuszkow, and Nancy Klusmeyer each ably typed portions of a difficult bilingual manuscript.

Finally, I should like to thank my parents, Herman and Nettie Geltman, for their loving support and respect for learning which set me on the path to scholarship.

Chronology

1901 Julian Przyboś born.
1911 Czesław Miłosz born.
1918– End of World War I; rebirth of independent Poland.
1919
1921 Birth of Krzysztof Kamil Baczyński and Tadeusz Róże-
      wicz.
1922 Birth of Tadeusz Gajcy and Miron Białoszewski.
1923 Wisława Szymborska born.
1924 Zbigniew Herbert born.
1925 Przyboś publishes first volume of poetry, *Śruby* (Screws).
1932 Przyboś, *W głąb las* (Into the Forest Depths).
1933 Miłosz publishes first volume of poetry, *Poemat o czasie
      zastygłem* (A Poem on Congealed Time). Jerzy Hara-
      symowicz born.
1934 Stanisław Grochowiak born.
1938 Przyboś, *Równanie serca* (Equation of the Heart).
1939 September 1, German invasion of Poland; beginning of
      World War II.
1942 Baczyński publishes *Wiersze wybrane* (Selected Poems)
      under pseudonym, Jan Bugaj.
1943 Gajcy publishes *Widma* (Specters) under pseudonym,
      Karol Topornicki. Baczyński, *Arkusz poetycki Jana Bugaja*
      (Jan Bugaj's Poetic Sheet).
1944 Gajcy, *Grom powszedni* (Daily Thunder). August 1–Octo-
      ber 3, the Warsaw Uprising. August 4, death of Baczyński.
      August 16, death of Gajcy.
1945 End of World War II. Miłosz, *Ocalenie* (Rescue). Przyboś,
      Miejsce na ziemi (A Place on Earth).
1947 Różewicz publishes first volume of poetry, *Niepokój*
      (Anxiety).
1947– Stalinization of Polish political and cultural life; imposi-
1955 tion of socialist realism in literature.
1951 Miłosz chooses exile.

1952 Szymborska publishes first volume of poetry, *Dlatego żyjemy* (That Is Why We Live).

1953 Miłosz, *Światło dzienne* (Daylight).

1955 Przyboś, *Najmniej słów* (The Fewest Possible Words).

1955– The post-Stalin "Thaw."
1956

1956 Różewicz, *Poemat otwarty* (An Open Poem). Each of the following publishes first volume of poetry: Białoszewski, *Obroty rzeczy* (Revolutions of Things); Grochowiak, *Ballada rycerska* (Knight's Ballad); Harasymowicz, *Cuda* (Miracles); Herbert, *Struna światła* (String of Light).

1957 Harasymowicz, *Powrót do kraju łagodności* (Return to the Land of Gentleness). Herbert, *Hermes, pies i gwiazda* (Hermes, a Dog and a Star). Miłosz, *Traktat poetycki* (Treatise on Poetry). Szymborska, *Wołanie do Yeti* (Crying to the Yeti).

1958 Grochowiak, *Menuet z pogrzebaczem* (Minuet With a Poker). Harasymowicz, *Wieża melancholii* (Tower of Melancholy). Przyboś, *Narzędzie ze światła* (Instrument of Light).

1959 Białoszewski, *Rachunek zachciankowy* (Whimsical Reckoning). Grochowiak, *Rozbieranie do snu* (Undressing for Sleep).

1960 Harasymowicz, *Mit o świętym Jerzym* (Myth of Saint George). Różewicz, *Rozmowa z księciem* (Conversation with the Prince).

1961 Białoszewski, *Mylne wzruszenia* (Mistaken Emotions). Herbert, *Studium przedmiotu* (Study of the Object). Przyboś, *Próba całości* (An Attempt at Wholeness). Różewicz, *Głos anonima* (Voice of Anonymous Man).

1962 Przyboś, *Więcej o manifest* (More Than a Manifesto). Różewicz, *Nic w płaszczu Prospera* (Nothing in Prospero's Cloak). Szymborska, *Sól* (Salt).

1963 Grochowiak, *Agresty* (Gooseberries).

1964 Różewicz, *Twarz* (Face).

1965 Białoszewski, *Było i było* (It Was and It Was). Przyboś, *Na znak* (As a Sign). Miłosz, *Gucio zaczarowany* ("Bobo's Metamorphosis").

1966 Harasymowicz, *Pastorałki polskie* (Polish Pastorals).

1967 Szymborska, *Sto pociech* (A Barrel of Laughs).
1969 Grochowiak, *Nie było lata* (There Was No Summer) and *Totentanz in Polen* (Dance of Death in Poland). Harasymowicz, *Madonny polskie* (Polish Madonnas). Herbert, *Napis* (Inscription). Miłosz, *Miasto bez imienia* (The City Without a Name). Przyboś, *Kwiat nieznany* (Unknown Flower). Różewicz, *Regio.*
1970 October 6, death of Julian Przyboś.
1971 Harasymowicz, *Znaki nad domen* (Signs Over the House).
1972 Harasymowicz, *Bar na Stawach* (Bar at the Ponds). Szymborska, *Wszelki wypadek* (In Any Event).
1974 Harasymowicz, *Żaglowiec* (The Sailboat). Herbert, *Pan Cogito* (Mr. Cogito). Miłosz, *Gdzie wschodzi słońce i kędy zapada* (Where the Sun Rises and Where It Sets).
1975 Grochowiak, *Bilard* (Billiards). Harasymowicz, *Barokowe czasy* (Baroque Times).
1976 September 2, death of Stanisław Grochowiak. Szymborska, *Wielka liczba* (Large Number).
1977 Różewicz, *Duszyczka* (Little Psyche).
1978 Grochowiak, *Haiku-images.* Harasymowicz, *Banderia prutenorum czyli Chorągwie pruskie podniesione roku pańskiego 1410* (Banderia prutenorum or Prussian Banners Raised Up in the Year of Our Lord 1410).

CHAPTER 1

Introduction to Contemporary
Polish Poetry

POETRY commands a special place in Polish culture. In a
nation which has long been subject to the malevolent designs
of powerful neighbors, poetry is more than a highly developed
art providing a refined aesthetic experience for an elite reader-
ship. Since at least the romantic era (the second quarter of the
nineteenth century), Poland's greatest poets have professed a
special calling which is also a special burden—to speak to and
for the nation in its times of agony and to record its trials in
their verse. Stylistic developments in Polish poetry have broadly
paralleled those in more familiar European literatures. The
themes of Polish poets are as varied as those of poets anywhere.
But the special characteristic which gives the poetry as a whole
its coherence is its unfailing attention to the national identity.

At different periods, depending on the history and politics
of the moment, Poland has been for her poets an object of venera-
tion, a society to be scorned, the incarnation of Christian martyr-
dom, or a tiresome burden. Polish poets contemplating the fate
of the Polish nation have sought a balance between their loyalty
to their poetic calling and their loyalty to their people. For
some, there has been no conflict; for others, the conflict has been
almost irreconcilable. The force of the tradition is strong, and
the question of poetry and Poland forces itself upon succeeding
generations of poets.

Generally speaking, nineteenth-century Polish poetry was
marked by a yearning for a Polish rebirth. Poland did not exist
as a nation; it had been partitioned by Russia, Prussia, and Austria
during the last quarter of the eighteenth century. In a sense, for
much of the nineteenth century poetry *was* the Polish nation.

17

The persistence of Polish literature (with poetry its dominant mode) was a living symbol of the existence of a Polish nation which some day, it was hoped, would again assume a geopolitical form.

That day came for Poland in the aftermath of World War I. For two decades, until the German occupation of Poland in 1939, an independent Polish state existed. For approximately one decade after this rebirth, the dominant mood of Polish poetry was euphoric. The awesome burden had been lifted from the shoulders of poets who could now turn away from contemplation of Poland's mysterious destiny and embrace more mundane themes of personal happiness and the ordinary experiences of ordinary people. This was what characterized Skamander, the spirited, popular poetic grouping which dominated Polish poetry during the interwar years. The poets who belonged to Skamander—among them such imposing figures as Julian Tuwim, Antoni Słonimski, Jarosław Iwaszkiewicz, Kazimierz Wierzyński—continued writing well into the post–World War II period.

The Skamander poets were opposed by at least two different avant-garde movements. The most prominent poet of the first of these avant-gardes was Julian Przyboś, a revolutionary in both his aesthetic beliefs and his political enthusiasms. Przyboś's insistent attention to metaphoric language, his manipulation of language to derive from it a multiplicity of meanings, has been an important precedent for younger poets such as Miron Białoszewski, who have, however, far outstripped him in their linguistic experimentations.

Czesław Miłosz is the most important poet of the second avant-garde and one of the major poets writing in any language today. Miłosz's original impact, in his poetry from the 1930s, was as a "Catastrophist"—a Cassandra who foresaw the coming convulsion of European culture. The crisis which he, among others, sensed, has become one of the central themes of postwar Polish poetry. As an émigré since 1951, Miłosz has been able to speak freely to his fellow Polish poets about the intricate entanglements of poetry and politics in our age. Among the poets writing in Poland today, Zbigniew Herbert is Miłosz's closest heir.

The crises of the 1930s (worldwide depression, the growth of totalitarianisms, omens of impending war) which sparked Przyboś's hopes for revolutionary upheaval and Miłosz's visions of catastrophe, came to a head in Poland on September 1, 1939. On that day the German armies opened their drive to the East by crossing the border with Poland. The weaker nation was quickly defeated by Nazi military power, and there ensued in Poland more than five years of brutal subjugation. Polish cultural life was driven underground and once again Polish poets became, by force of circumstance, defenders of the nation's will to exist.

During the dread years of the Nazi occupation two young poets of great promise made their literary debuts, only to lose their lives within a few brief years. Tadeusz Gajcy and Krzysztof Kamil Baczyński were among the most gifted members of the rising generation of poets which found itself in thrall to history in a way that no preceding generation of Polish poets had known. Both these young poets perished in 1944 during the fighting in the Warsaw Uprising.

The most significant poets of contemporary Poland belong to the generation of writers who, like Gajcy and Baczyński, began their literary careers while Poland was under the Nazi occupation. Survivors of the debacle of European civilization, these writers—Tadeusz Różewicz, Wisława Szymborska, Miron Białoszewski, Zbigniew Herbert—all are scarred in one way or another by their experience of Nazi warfare and the Stalinist Communism which quickly succeeded it in Poland. As poets, these four are distinct individuals with characteristic styles and obsessions. They are linked by the fact that the crucial event for them personally and for their poetry was their wartime experience, which forced them to question the viability of poetic traditions and the sometimes competing obligations of the poet to his gift and his society.

Among the younger established poets there has been a swing away from the war guilt which has been such an obsessive theme in Polish poetry since 1945. Jerzy Harasymowicz and Stanisław Grochowiak, like the older Białoszewski and Herbert, made their debuts in 1956, the year which marked the loosening of Communist political control over Polish literature. For somewhat less than a decade before this, Polish literature had been subject to the withering dictates of socialist realism with its stern prescription of joy, simplicity, and phony moral uplift, enforced by censorship and harsh sanctions. In the mid-1950s, in the aftermath of Stalin's death, writers again found it possible to speak, with a certain degree of freedom, of the crises through which the nation had passed, and to turn their art in directions not prescribed by Party directives. Harasymowicz immersed himself in quaint regional folklore and fanciful legends of Poland's past. Grochowiak, in contrast, took the war generation's distrust of traditional values even further in his deliberate search for ugliness and discord.

The most recent generation of poets—those who were born after the war and made their debuts beginning in the mid-1960s —has been attacked by some Polish critics as apathetic and bland. It is still too early, however, to assess the role of this generation in the future development of Polish poetry.

CHAPTER 2

Julian Przyboś: Undaunted Optimist

THE literary career of Julian Przyboś spans almost half a
century, from its beginnings in the avant-garde movement
of the early 1920s until his death in 1970. It was a career marked
by paradox. Born into a conservative peasant family, Przyboś
became an ardent enthusiast of technological innovation and
proletarian revolution. A firm believer in the writer's duty to
speak out on behalf of revolutionary change, he was also an
aesthete whose difficult poetry was written for an audience of
poets, not workers. A representative of the avant-garde, he was
honored by Poland's Communist regime and became a member
of the literary establishment under a government whose official
policy was to support only staid socialist realism in the arts.

I *Biographical Note*

Julian Przyboś was born in 1901 in the village of Gwoźnica,
near the provincial town of Rzeszów in the flat lands of south-
eastern Poland, which was part of the Austro-Hungarian empire
during his childhood and youth. Although from a peasant family,
Przyboś was not an untutored "natural" peasant poet. After
graduating from the provincial high school, he enrolled in
Cracow's Jagiellonian University in 1920.

This was a time of great intellectual ferment in Poland. The
state had only recently been reconstituted by provisions of the
Versailles Treaty, and the general spirit of jubilation aroused
by the long-awaited national rebirth was accompanied by an
openness toward new social and artistic ideas. Among the many
competing currents of thought, the young Przyboś was particularly attracted to radical theories derived in part from Italian

21

and Russian futurism and constructivism. He became affiliated
with a movement led by the poet and theoretician Tadeusz
Peiper. Peiper's program, with its futurist glorification of technological development (even more of a wistful absurdity in
sleepy Cracow than in prerevolutionary Russia), called for
rigorous form, the abandonment of purely decorative effects in
poetry, and a thematic concentration on the "three *m*'s" of
contemporary life: metropolis, masses, machine (*miasto, masa,
maszyna*).[1] These were to be the basic themes of Przyboś's
early poetry.

After completing university studies in literature, Przyboś
became a high school teacher. He continued as an active member of the literary avant-garde, contributing to and collaborating
on a number of journals during the 1920s and 1930s. He spent
the years 1937–1939 in Paris on a fellowship, expanding his
horizons by this first contact with a major metropolis and center
of European culture.

After spending roughly the first year and a half of World War
II in the Soviet Union (in Polish territory annexed by the
Russians), Przyboś returned to his native village in 1941, pre-
tending to be a peasant in order to evade the Nazi terror directed against Polish intellectuals and radicals. When the Red
Army advanced into eastern Poland during the summer of 1944,
he offered his services to the Soviet-sponsored Lublin provi-
sional government. From then on he was active as a leading
spirit in a number of Communist-backed cultural enterprises,
particularly the newly organized Union of Writers and the
literary journal *Odrodzenie* (Rebirth).

One problem plaguing the new postwar Polish government
was the lack of trained personnel who could serve at the
higher levels of government. The corps of foreign-service officers,
created out of whole cloth after 1918, had been decimated
during the war by both German and Soviet terrorism and was
further reduced by the decision of many Poles to remain in exile
in opposition to the new regime. In these circumstances, Przyboś
was appointed ambassador to Switzerland, where he served
from 1947 through 1951. His appointment was doubly advan-
tageous: the new Polish government gained in being repre-

sented by a highly cultured intellectual, and the new ambassador was safely removed from a country where publication of his more complex poetry was a political impossibility.

During the last decade and a half of his life Przyboś lived in Warsaw. The obscure, avant-garde teacher-poet of the twenties and thirties ended his life as a member of the literary establishment, famous for his fine essays in literary criticism, as well as for his poetry, and renowned for his bitter, sometimes vicious denunciations of the post-1956 generation of poets. He died of a heart attack in October, 1970.

II *Early Works*

During his long literary career Przyboś's poetry exhibited numerous changes in themes and perspective.[2] Nonetheless, certain characteristic enthusiasms and obsessions span the fifty years of his creative life. Chief among these are an obsessive fascination with sources of light and energy, an attraction to skewed spatial perspectives, a concern for the expansion of the literary text through full exploitation of sound instrumentation and multiple meanings, and a programmatic optimism about the future of mankind. In all his poetry he is committed to renewing perception of reality through the use of striking metaphors.

Although he eventually was to deny the value of his earliest poetry, all these interests can be found in Przyboś's first two collections of poems, *Śruby* (Screws, 1925) and *Oburącz* (With Both Hands, 1926).[3] Both *Screws* and *With Both Hands* are startlingly aggressive celebrations of technology and of the city as the incarnation of mechanical and human energy—a theme which had been in general currency in Europe since the early years of the century. Przyboś is filled with an almost hysterical enthusiasm for the whirling tempo of city life; his poems vibrate to the pulsating energy of generators and factories.

The poem "Roofs" may serve as a laboratory in which to examine many of Przyboś's motifs and poetic devices. It is a paean to the city, which Przyboś perceives not as a composite of geometrical solids or the static enclosure of a human community, but as a dynamic, barely constrainable force in perpetual, con-

vulsive motion. "Roofs" opens with a shout and rises, in its first
few lines, to a frenzied crescendo:[4]

> Higher!
> Twisted planes, multi-storied pyramids,
> spinning planes, soaring planes,
> form-creating.
> Contortion
> of massive space,
> spasms
> of cities being born.

Wyżej! / Płaszczyzny kręte, piramidy pięter, / płaszczyzny wirujące,
płaszczyzny wznoszące, / figurotwórcze. / Masywnej przestrzeni /
skręt, / rodzących się miast / kurcze.

The translator of Przyboś's poetry is frequently confronted
with the impossibility of suggesting in one English equivalent
the multiple meanings contained in particular Polish words or
suggested by the context in which they are placed. Here, however, English perversely offers a double meaning, Polish only
one. "Płaszczyzny" ("planes") means only a two-dimensional surface and does not, in Polish, have any relation to flying machines.
With this caveat in mind, let us proceed to a closer examination
of this fragment.

In these tightly structured lines Przyboś is attempting to
render in verse the seething energy of a city perceived from
above. The only full sentence is the one-word command: "Higher!"
The verbal forms are dynamic active participles, formed from
verbs which denote convulsive action, as do two of the nouns
(*skręt*—"contortion"; *kurcze*—"spasms"). The text is rich in al-
literation, particularly of the plosive sound *p*. Rhyme is used
only occasionally and at greater distances (five lines) than is
usual in more traditional prosody, and also in approximate form
(pięter / skręt; figurotwórcze / kurcze). It is significant that the
two rhymes are based on the two violent nouns. The contortion
of movement is emphasized by the use of internal rhyme (kręte /
pięter; wirujące / wznoszące), by syntactic inversion, and by the
repetition of individual words and entire syntactic structures.
All this contributes to the extraordinary tension of the poem

which ends with an exhortation to the city literally to soar to the skies.

The explosive potential of the city is dramatized in poem after poem in both *Screws* and *With Both Hands*. Using imagery which appears to echo the hyperbole of Majakovskij's revolutionary poems, Przyboś predicts a city-based revolution of almost cosmic proportions. Yet despite his espousal in his early poetry of the goals of a proletarian revolution, the distinct impression is that the workers in Przyboś's poems really exist to illustrate the might of machines, rather than as beneficiaries of those marvels of technology. Przyboś sings the praises of electrification in his poem "Dynamo," for example, but it is the sheer energy of generators rather than their social utility which attracts him.[5] Electrical energy is exciting because it is potentially destructive as well as constructive, and this negative attraction is expressed through violent metaphors:[6]

> The brute force
> of electricity exploded
> like golden vomit
> from black jaws.

Z czarnych paszcz / złotym womitem / gwałt / elektryczności buchnął.

Although Przyboś's extreme enthusiasm for the city was soon tempered, his obsession with energy persisted, and his attraction to convulsive social movements continued to be expressed in his poems on political themes.

III *Political Poems*

In the 1920s and 1930s, Przyboś was among the powerless minority who espoused the cause of proletarian revolution in Poland. In his poem of advice to a younger colleague, "Letter," he expressed his dissatisfaction with his poet's role of mere inciter to revolutionary activity:[7]

> Constructing yourself, you incite the foundations to revolt!
> In anger, I

have forced the gates with every period;
you
will blast them from the wall with a bomb.

Budując siebie, burzysz podziemia do buntu! / Ja—z gniewu / każdą
kropką wysadzałem bramy, / ty / bombą powysadzasz je z muru.

Przyboś's own poetic bombshells are often quite crude. One
of his strongest denunciations of the capitalist class is the versi-
fied lampoon "Menu." In it Przyboś depicts a monstrous bourgeois glutton with a hundred mouths stuffing himself with hunks
of meat until his churning stomach erupts, spewing its contents
over the table while the obsequious waiters dance attendance.[8]
This is one of his more peculiar variations on the theme of
explosive energy.

While other Polish writers during the 1930s had terrifying
forebodings of the imminent upheaval in Europe, Przyboś, politically less astute than they, yearned for the anticipated con-
flagration.[9] In the title poem of *Równanie serca* (Equation of
the Heart, 1938), which was published virtually on the eve of
the Nazi assault on Europe, Przyboś gave voice to this state of
expectancy:[10]

> The people, up in arms, are laying dynamite
> under all the triumphal arches!
> .   .   .   .
> The table, having swollen under my pen to its very rim,
> overflows its bounds
> like a tank poised for attack.
> The house is already aflame inside me today with
>   tomorrow's conflagration,
> my heart is attacking me in haste.

Pod wszystkie triumfalne bramy / zbuntowani podkładają dyna-
mit! / / . . . / / Stół pod moim piórem wezbrawszy do samych kraw-
ędzi / przebiera swą miarę, / jak czołg, gdy ma ruszyć do ataku. /
Dom już dziś płonie we mnie jutrzejszym pożarem, / serce atakuje
mię prędzej.

Przyboś appears to have been somewhat chastened but not
devastated by the experience of World War II. His extraordinary

optimism buoyed him up even in the midst of national disaster. What is most striking about *Póki my żyjemy* (While We Live, 1944), his collection of war poems, is its relatively sanguine tone. This is not to say that Przyboś was impervious to his nation's suffering or that the catastrophic events of war and occupation are not reflected in his poetry. "At the Crest of the Road," for example, with its striking images of automobiles fleeing on reserves of terror when their gas supplies are exhausted, of soldiers marching in their own funeral processions, is just one of a number of poems which he wrote in direct response to the Nazi terror. Przyboś is not being disingenuous when he says in this poem, "I still feel the despair of that shame today: that I survived" ("Jeszcze dziś czuję rozpacz tego wstydu: żem—przeżył").[11]

Poems of grief, however, are outnumbered by works which reflect the author's irrepressible optimism. In "Spring 1941" and "Spring 1942" Przyboś wrote without horror or despair about nature's renewal in the midst of all the carnage on Earth.[12] As we shall see, nature's abundant fertility, unaffected by the decimation of mankind, is a frequent theme for Polish poets during the war and postwar period. The common reaction is one of revulsion against the indecent blind life-force. Przyboś is virtually alone in his celebration of life amid the carnage. In "Autumn 1942" he attempted to justify (to himself?) his continuing joy in life and his pacific occupation as a poet:[13]

> Extermination is imminent!
> but I draw down an apple bough:
> I hide myself in awe . . .
>
> . . . .
> When the day is like a one-day delay in the execution
>   of a sentence
> I fill it the more fruitfully with life
> unto the depths of night.
> I catch your terror in lightning peace, as in a trap.
> I take part in the common struggle—
> alone.

Nadciąga zagłada! / a ja kłonię gałąź jabłoni: / ukrywam się w podziwie . . . / / Gdy dzień—jak odroczenie na dzień wykonaniu wyroku, /

tym owocniej wypełniam go życiem / do dna nocy. / Chwytam wasz
strach, jak w potrzask, w błyskawiczny spokój. / Osobno—w walce
spółnoty / biorę udział.

Although Przyboś enlisted in "the common struggle" to build
a socialist state after the war, he did not attempt to turn his
poetry into a weapon. There are a few perhaps obligatory poems
from the Stalinist years which are openly propagandistic. These
include "Letter to My Brother in the Country,"[14] an appeal to
the peasants to accept collectivization and the mechanization
of agriculture, and "New Cracow,"[15] a poem in praise of the
construction of the planned industrial city of Nowa Huta, a
short distance from medieval Cracow. The imagery of this latter
poem is so trite as to give rise to the suspicion that it was
written to orders—actual or self-imposed. However, "Spring
1956," in which Przyboś allies himself with the anti-Stalinist
political movement, is equally trite, depending on images of
breaking ice, sun arising from darkness, etc.[16] It, too, is written
with a militant enthusiasm which makes it indistinguishable in
style from Przyboś's Stalinist construction poems, although its
political message is diametrically opposed to theirs.

Ideologically and temperamentally Przyboś seemed suited
to be a writer of noisy rhetorical poems. His exuberant vitality,
his faith in technology and in the revolutionary restructuring of
society inclined him in his early poetry toward the type of poetic
statement which achieves its effect by piling one exaggerated
exclamation upon another. Although he once defined a poet as
"an exclamation point of the street,"[17] Przyboś was essentially
too much of an aesthete to be satisfied with loudness devoid of
poetic quality. Despite the self-imposed pressures of his own
ideology, he remained faithful to his poetic principles in the
vast body of his work.

IV Private Themes

Przyboś's determined optimism (which at times is so insistent
as to seem the product of some grim compulsion) yielded opposing results in his public and private poems. In the former,
his ardent enthusiasms often produce a disquieting political

obtuseness and verse deformed by stridency and a decided lack
of subtlety. In the private lyric poems, however, this same
openness to life's promises often results in works of great sensual vividness and emotional delicacy.

Many of Przyboś's most interesting poems incorporate descriptions of the Polish landscape which, beginning with the
volume *W głąb las* (Into the Forest Depths, 1932), appears as
a physical reality and as the embodiment of metaphysical di-
lemmas as well. Delineated by tree-lined roads or gently rolling
hills, his landscapes appear to be faithful pictures of a finite
reality. But they are also clearly the poet's private creation, since
the choice of perspective is always his. Przyboś frequently
manipulates the illusory quality imparted to space by visual
perspective, dependent as it is on distance, topographical con-
tours, and play of lights. In his poems the open spaces of the
countryside are fraught with menace as well as promise. A
village may glow with expectancy as in "Cottages," where the
sun-splashed peasant huts appear to be the seed-centers of
radiant sunflowers and where even the pitchforks stand ex-
pectantly beside the cottage doors.[18] Alternately, the very boun-
tifulness of the fertile earth may be asphyxiating. "I am choking
on the excess of this world," Przyboś gasps in "On the Road"
("Krztuszę się świata nadmiarem").[19]

A new form of landscape depiction is achieved in the Paris
poems which are found in *Equation of the Heart* and the retrospective postwar collection, *Miejsce na ziemi* (A Place on
Earth, 1945). The best of these are a happy blend of vibrant
enthusiasm for the cosmopolitan capital and a nostalgic yearning for the Polish village. In "Since Last Year," one of the most
lyrical of the Paris poems, the French capital is seen through
the prism of a nostalgic yearning for the Polish countryside
and for a loved woman who remains at home. Przyboś conveys
this dual perspective by describing ordinary aspects of the city
scene in terms of homely rural metaphors:[20]

> I walk through this same different city,
> impassive,
> in flight from myself,
> and along a broad street across an empty field I lead
> a mechanical horse.

. . . . . .
From your distant garden
I stoop to pluck
here,
on the gleaming, mirrored asphalt,
a dew-sprinkled bouquet of electric
asters.

Idę tym samym miastem innym, / od siebie odbiegłym, / głuchym, / i wiodę pustym polem po ulicy szczerej / mechanicznego konia. / / . . . / / Z dalekiego twojego ogrodu / schylam się, aby zerwać / tu, / na świetlistych źwierciadlanych asfaltach, / zroszony bukiet elektrycznych / astrów.

In "Since Last Year" both time and space are displaced for the speaker of the poem. More commonly, however, space alone is manipulated in Przyboś's poetry. "Notre Dame" (the first of three poems on the great cathedral) is an interesting example of Przyboś's presentation of spatial perception from an unexpected viewpoint.[21] Here, of course, the space perceived has been narrowed from a land- or cityscape to a single edifice. Looking at the cathedral from a height at least equal to its own, he observes with terror the soaring vastness of its interior space. He is awed by the menacing gargoyles and humbled by the immensity of this structure raised by unknown craftsmen. Though his poem begins with almost conventional exclamations of wonder—"Oh space which soars from a million fingers poised in prayer!" ("Z miliona złożonych do modlitwy palców wzlatująca przestrzeń!")—it ends, after a meditation on death, with a sudden and brilliant reversal of perspective which captures the horror of the void evoked by the cathedral: "Who thought up this abyss and flung it on high!" ("Kto pomyślał tę przepaść i odrzucił ją w górę!") "Notre-Dame" is also notable as one of Przyboś's rare prewar meditative poems. The suppressed fears of death alluded to in this work only began to gain prominence in Przyboś's poetry some two decades later.

As previously noted, Przyboś's poetry is suffused with an enthusiastic affirmation of life. The obsessive nature of this enthusiasm is apparent from the ritual series of spring poems beginning with "Spring 1934" and ending with "Spring 1970" in which, with rare exceptions, Przyboś finds a source of hope in nature's annual rebirth. The delight in life is coupled, however, with an insatiable yearning for experience and a fear of being unable to live life to the fullest. The shadow cast by the radiant energy of so much of Przyboś's poetry can be perceived in a single punning phrase which also aptly illustrates his principle of wringing a multiplicity of meaning from every verse:[22]

> Truly, awe appears only once.
> It appeared to me in my pastoral childhood
> as a sign:
> Exist!
> I live in wonder.

Dziw się zjawia tylko raz prawdziwie. / Zjawił mi się w pastuszym dzieciństwie / na znak: / Istniej! / Żyję w podziwie.

The key words here are in the last line. The literal meaning of "w podziwie" is "in wonder" or "in awe," but analyzed into their component parts (w + po + dziw [ie]), these words can also be taken to mean "in after-awe" or "in after-wonder"—a state of deprivation after the original moment of epiphany.[23] In these ambiguities the duality of Przyboś's life-affirming poetry is captured: it is a celebration of life which is in part a frantic escape from the knowledge that life is a constant dying away as well as a constant renewal.

V *The Shadow of Death*

During the late 1950s, the search for the original source of that compound of wonder and terror became one of the major themes of Przyboś's poetry. From a fascination with the varieties of spatial perspectives in the world around him, he turned to an exploration of his inner self. Combining the insights of psychoanalysis with a poet's license to create his own mythology, Przyboś identified two primal events in his earliest childhood: his first vision of radiant sunlight and his learning that a baby sister had burned to death before he was born.

In "Living," Przyboś recreates the moment when he rose from a crawling posture to face the bright glow of sunlight in

the sky. All of life since that moment, he asserts, has been a
yearning toward that instant of dazzling clarity, an effort at
recapturing its splendid promise through his poetry.[24] Hence,
the central importance of light in his *oeuvre*. As he wrote in the
poem "Introduction to Poetics":[25]

> my word is photosensitive
> and grows quieter
> when the sun does not shine
> . . . .
> I watch for the word to rise and once
>   more shine forth, clarified by light,
> light changed by speech into the word.

moje słowo jest światłoczułe i staje się cichsze, / kiedy słońce nie świeci. / . . . . / patrzę, kiedy się wzniesie i znów pojaśnieje słowo ob-
jaśnione przez światło, / światło wmówione w słowo.

Przyboś explored the negative source of his ambivalent fascination with light and energy—his sister's death by fire—in one of
his most expressive meditative poems, "The World Recedes,"
from the collection *Próba całości* (An Attempt at Wholeness,
1961).[26] Here the poet speaks of his sense that time is passing
beyond his grasp. He who used to celebrate the strength of
matter and yearn only for more power, more energy, more speed,
can now no longer feel delight untainted by horror ("i we mnie
dziś / nie ma / zachwytu bez przerażenia"). The poet locates
the source of his anxieties in his early childhood. He describes
a visit to his native village when he suddenly finds himself able
to reach back to his earliest memories, locating among them
"the embryonic archetype of imagination." This is revealed to
be his discovery of the facts surrounding the death of the sister
he never knew. The flames of the bonfire which took her life,
he asserts, left their emotional scars on the child who succeeded
her—the author. Przyboś achieves a resolution of sorts by reflecting on his own child's current happiness. In these same fields
where his sister's tragic death occurred, his little daughter Uta
runs gaily through the grass, delighting in the same sensations
as the author half a century before.

Unfortunately, space does not permit an extended discussion of

Przyboś's poems to this daughter, Uta. These works reveal a lyric tenderness which is rarely evinced in his poetry. They are also extremely interesting from the standpoint of wordplay. Making use of a child's free construction of grammatical forms based on a logical application of the rules of grammar, Przyboś experiments with language and fantasy more freely in these pieces than anywhere else. Some of his poems to Uta are reminiscent of Julian Tuwim's linguistic experimentation in his "słopiewnie." Others, such as the charming and clever "Hide-and-seek"[27] are disguised philosophical meditations.

In his late middle age, Przyboś's youngest daughter was an important focus of his life-affirming optimism, deflecting his attention from his personal obsessive fears. In the last decade or so of his life, however, a new source of terror surfaced as a theme to be explored in his poetry. It is the inescapable recognition of the duality of body and spirit as the body begins to fail long before the greedy spirit is willing to relinquish its hold on life. Not based on private mythologies or obsessions, these poems on the universal themes of old age and infirmity move closer to a pure lyricism than any of Przyboś's earlier works.

"Last Year's Verse," for example, is an irritable dialogue between the poet's spirit (the "I" of the poem) and his corporeal self (addressed as an alien "you").[28] The spirit affirms that life is not short if one can approach it through word-art and that joy (or "lightness") is the antidote for sorrow. (Again a pun: "Na najcięższy ze smutków zamiast *leku*–/lekkość"; "For the heaviest of sorrows instead of medicine–/lightness.") But the body claims its due nonetheless, and its frailty poses a question which the spirit cannot answer:

> Without a single ray of light
> how can one impart to a phrase that speed close to light,
> how can one conquer time?

Bez jednego promienia / jak nadać zdaniu prędkość zbliżoną do światła, / jak czas zwyciężać?

Przyboś maintained to the very end a delicate balance between grief at his own mortality and his more natural expansiveness in response to the eternal self-renewal of earth. He posed this as a riddle in the intriguing late poem, "Mostar":[29]

> The world begins but is not completed?
> It neither exists nor doesn't not exist?
> Eternal uncertainty, a constant Between,
> what we call Existence—*is*?

Świat się zaczyna, nie spełnia? / Ani nie istnieje, ani nie nie istnieje? / Wieczna niepewność, ustawiczne Między, / to, co zowiemy Bytem— jest że?

Eventually he accepted each passing year, however hampered by illness, as a triumph of survival, and found cause for wonder even in his partially crippled life. There is a touching pathos in his revised definitions of wonder ("dziw"):[30]

> That I transported across the drifts and snowstorms
>   of this long winter
> to this spring
> of suddenly riotous flowers
> my heavy naked heart . . .
> that this anaemic muscle still contracts,
> expands again . . .
> This is wondrous. . . .

Że przeniosłem z długiej zimy przez jej zaspy i śnieżyce / do tej wiosny / we gwałtownych, wszystkich naraz kwiatach / ciężkie moje obnażone serce . . . / że ten niedokrwiony mięsień kurczy się, / rozkurcza się jeszcze . . . / To dziw. . . .

VI *Conclusion*

Julian Przyboś entered Polish poetry at a time of considerable ferment and experimentation, aligning himself with the most radical wing of the avant-garde movement. Throughout his almost fifty years of poetic practice he remained faithful to his basic principle, that poetry must renew the reader's perceptions by means of strikingly juxtaposed metaphors based on an explosion of verbal signification.

A major goal of his poetry is the search for a poetic language which is both stripped of traditional accretions which blunt the senses and, at the same time, is comprehensible. To achieve an effect of fresh perception he frequently resorts to startling imagery and deliberate manipulation of normal angles of observation in his highly visual poetry. His poems, seeking to maximize the multiplicity of meanings inherent in any word's echoes (through etymology, close rhyme words, puns, neologistic extensions of meaning) are often actually quite difficult. They are also, because of this stylistic feature, peculiarly resistant to translation. Whether Przyboś actually succeeded in achieving his goals remains a controversial question. He is generally acknowledged to be a poet's poet, whose work is simply too difficult to attract the large audience he professed to seek.

Although Przyboś began his poetic career as a rebel against traditional aesthetic standards, at the end of his life he assumed a position of implacable hostility toward the most extreme manifestations of linguistic and thematic innovation in postwar Polish poetry. Nevertheless, his own example as an innovator who boldly pursued his own themes and private obsessions contributed in no small part to the stylistic freedom which the post-1956 avant-garde was to exploit in a variety of ways. Ultimately, Przyboś's quarrel with these younger poets can be attributed as much to a question of world outlook as of aesthetics. The postwar generation looks upon the world, as we shall see, as a place devoid of eternal values and insists on celebrating its ugliness and squalor. Not even the experience of two devastating world wars could undercut Przyboś's basic optimism. To the end his verse was dedicated to a celebration of his vision of a radiant universe and the inevitable progress of mankind toward a better future.

CHAPTER 3

Czesław Miłosz: Poetry and Ethics

THE life and literary career of Czesław Miłosz present a
striking illustration of the extent to which historical experience has affected the individual destinies of Poland's contemporary poets. He cannot be comprehended apart from the context
of the chaotic upheavals in Eastern European society during this
century. Miłosz has described his own poetry quite aptly as a
fusion of "individual and historical elements . . . an alloy that one
seldom encounters in the West."[1] Like T. S. Eliot and W. H.
Auden, in his classically restrained poetry Miłosz addresses the
crucial problems of the twentieth century: the cataclysms of
world war, the destruction of cultural values, the crisis of religious
faith, the erosion of humaneness and individual dignity.

The international significance of Miłosz's poetry was first
recognized in 1978, when he was awarded the Neustadt International Prize for Literature, presented by the University of
Oklahoma. This honor was followed two years later by the
highest form of recognition—the awarding to Miłosz of the 1980
Nobel Prize for Literature.

I Bibliographical Note

Miłosz was born in 1911 in provincial Lithuania, an area that
had once been part of the great Polish–Lithuanian Republic but
which, in 1911, belonged to Russia. (After World War I Lithuania became an independent state, only to be occupied once
more in 1940 by Russian—now Soviet—forces.) Miłosz's writings
reveal his deep affection for both the pine-forested Lithuanian
landscape and the primitive local folk culture, so different from
the narrowly defined "Polishness" to which the Polish landowners
in Lithuania clung. In his autobiography *Rodzinna Europa*

(Native Realm) and his novel *Dolina Issy* (Valley of the Issa)[2] he portrayed these people as a culturally and economically impoverished class. From his youth Miłosz has retained a feeling of revulsion against the ethnic-Polish chauvinism, close-minded Catholicism, and mindless anti-Semitic feelings which he observed among the class of Polish landowners. A deep ambivalence about what it means to be a Pole contributes to that need to seek "self-definition" which is expressed in Miłosz's autobiographical works.

Miłosz was educated first in provincial Lithuania and then in the city of Wilno where he studied law at the centuries-old Stefan Batory University. There he became affiliated with several other young poets who, in 1931, founded the literary journal *Żagary* (Brushwood). This grouping was part of what is now referred to as the second wave of the interwar Polish literary avant-garde. In 1934–1935 Miłosz lived in Paris where his relative, the French poet Oscar V. de L. Miłosz, took him under his wing.[3] After his year abroad Miłosz went to work for Polish Radio. During the war he was active in the Warsaw literary underground.

Like Przyboś, Miłosz was tapped for diplomatic service by the new Polish government. In 1946 he came to America as a cultural attaché; in 1950 he assumed a comparable position in the Paris embassy. During this period he found himself increasingly uncomfortable as an official representative of a country whose recently liberated cultural elite was being manipulated and oppressed for the sake of alien political demands as the Russian-controlled Polish Communists assumed full power in the new state.

The alternatives available to Miłosz in these circumstances were all odious in one way or another. He could continue as a representative of the Polish government, but the price would be his sense of personal integrity and the ceding of control over his art to Stalinist censors. He could slip into the silence of "internal emigration"—a path chosen by a number of his contemporaries. He could break with his country and go into exile to face the cutting of his living tie with the Polish language and the loss of an audience attuned to the historical problems which concerned him.

Had Miłosz not been posted in America he might have broken

with the Communist regime at an earlier date. America, however, with its lack of direct experience of war, its postwar prosperity and naive optimism did not offer a congenial alternative. Miłosz renounced his affiliation with Poland's Communist regime in early 1951 and spent the remainder of the 1950s in France.[4] In 1960 he was appointed Professor of Slavic Literatures at the University of California at Berkeley—a position from which he recently retired. He has written some of his most impressive poetry during the past quarter century and has also published three novels, numerous essays on social and ethical themes, translations from French and English into Polish, translations into English of his own poetry and that of contemporary poets in Poland, and, in English, a textbook history of Polish literature.[5]

II   *Premonitions of Catastrophe: Poetry of the Thirties*

Miłosz began publishing his poetry in the early 1930s. The prewar poetry is represented by two volumes, *Poemat o czasie zastyg-łym* (Poem on Congealed Time, 1933) and *Trzy zimy* (Three Winters, 1936). This early poetry is marked thematically by an acute awareness of approaching catastrophe, both personal and universal. The themes of mutability and death explored in these early poems were to become major subjects of Miłosz's poetic *oeuvre*. Many of these early pieces are quite ponderous in form, betraying a beginning writer, but in a few of them the mature poet can already be discerned. The poem addressed "To Father Ch.," one of the most successful from this period despite its lapses into overblown rhetoric, illustrates both Miłosz's catastrophic premonitions and the discursive style of his philosophical poems:[6]

> The world trembles, the trees fall silent, when a just
>   man walks,
> but this too sinful age will bring forth no saint
> —thus you taught us; a stream of boiling lava
> will extinguish the cities and Noah will not escape in his
>   ark.
>
> .   .   .   .

We are reconciled after long antagonism,
knowing that not a stone will remain standing
of human happiness,
The earth will stretch wide its jaws and in its echoing
    cathedral
the last pagans will be baptized.

Ziemia drży, drzewo milknie, kiędy stąpa prawy, / ale wiek nazbyt
grzeszny świętego nie zrodzi / —tak uczyłeś, a miasta strumień
wrzącej lawy / zgasi i żaden Noe nie ujdzie na łodzi. / / . . . / /
Pogodzeni jesteśmy po długim skłóceniu, / wiedząc, że z szczęścia
ludzi kamień na kamieniu / nie zostanie. / Ziemia usta rozewrze, w
jej dudniącej katedrze / chrzest odbiorą ostatni poganie.

III *Witness to Apocalypse: Poetry of the War Years*

The German invasion of Poland on September 1, 1939, put
an end to premonitions. During the ensuing years of war and
occupation, Miłosz's anxiously prophetic voice yielded place to
the muted, sometimes strangled voice of an eyewitness reacting
to the dread present. Like the Polish romantics of the nineteenth
century and the youngest writers during the occupation (but
without their fervor and optimistic bravado), Miłosz adopted the
view that the poet is duty-bound to serve the nation as a moral
force. Poetry represented a personal indulgence, too; it provided
a means of confronting the ongoing horror with words of despair
and hatred and of escape into the happiness which once could
be found on earth but now could be created only by the poet's
imagination.

Ocalenie (Rescue, 1945), the collection of Miłosz's poetry
written during the war years, is resonant with the tension between
these opposing needs. In poems such as "Pastoral Song" or "The
World: A Naive Poem," Miłosz painted luminous pictures of a
gentle rural world and the harmony of family life. He defended
these flights from oppressive reality in "The Land of Poetry":[7]

Accept your invitation to that land,
Do not ask what it is called today,

You know what bitter shadows one
walks among there.
Is it a happy land? I do not know.

. . . .

That land is joined with pain forever
And sorrow alone can open its gates.

Do tej krainy przyjmij zaproszenie, / Nie pytaj, jak się dziś ona
nazywa, / Wiesz, przez jakie gorzkie tam idzie się cienie. / Czy jest
szczęśliwa? Nie wiem, czy szczęśliwa. / . . . / Z bólem na zawsze
ta ziemia złączona / I tylko smutek jej brama otwiera.

"The Land of Poetry" is a defensive apology for indulgence in
lyric poetry on private themes. Miłosz, like many other writers
at the time, had ambivalent feelings about the propriety of
writing poetry at a time of unprecedented suffering. In "The
Poor Poet" he speaks with revulsion of the urge to hide from
reality in self-created never-never lands of political fantasy,
alcoholic haze, or poetry. His disdain for those who have what
he calls "the hope of fools, rosy as erotic dreams" is matched only
by his self-contempt. He still cannot control his poet's impulse
to write of joyous worlds, but the civic part of him that functions
as ethical censor is appalled by such verse:[8]

The first movement is singing,
A free voice, filling mountains and valleys.
The first movement is joy,
But it is taken away.

. . . .

I poise the pen and it puts forth twigs and leaves, it is
covered with blossoms
And the scent of that tree is impudent, for there, on the
real earth,
Such trees do not grow, and like an insult
To suffering humanity is the scent of that tree.

Pierwszy ruch jest śpiewanie, / Swobodny głos napełniający góry i
doliny. / Pierwszy ruch jest radość, / Ale ona zostaje odjęta. / / . . .
/ / Stawiam pióro, i puszcza pędy i liście, okrywa się kwiatem, / A
zapach tego drzewa jest bezwstydny, bo tam, na realnej ziemi / Takie

drzewa nie rosną i jest jak zniewaga / Wyrządzona cierpiącym ludziom zapach tego drzewa.

The poet's self-condemnation is also clearly tinged with regret. The anonymous joy-destroying force in the shape of history has made poetry, too, its victim.

By the middle of the war the balance scale of Miłosz's verse had tipped from affirmation of life toward embroilment in death. Among the several excellent works which he composed about the destruction around him, his poem on the devastation of the Warsaw Ghetto in April, 1943—"A Poor Christian Looks at the Ghetto"—is, perhaps, the most striking.[9] In it Miłosz avoids the twin pitfalls of inappropriate and inadequate pathos by creating a nightmare image of a Jewish patriarch-guardian mole who picks his way among the bodies of the dead to stop finally at the poet's body, marked forever by the brand of noncircumcision as "one among the helpers of death." "A Poor Christian Looks at the Ghetto" is an unusually dramatic poem, quivering with the tensions created by terse enumerations of the materials destroyed in the ghetto flames, by the image of the mole, and by the mesmerizing chant of horror with which the poem opens: "Bees build around red liver,/Ants build around black bone."

More commonly, Miłosz approaches themes of ominous import with either the icy quiet of scathing irony or with deceptively placid description. "A Song on the End of the World" provides a good example of this falsely serene mode. The day the world ends, he writes, will be a day like any other. Bees will be gathering honey, sparrows splashing in rain gutters, people going about their ordinary occupations:[10]

> And those who expected lightning and thunder
> Are disappointed.
> And those who expected signs and archangels' trumps
> Do not believe it is happening now.
> As long as the sun and the moon are above,
> As long as the bumblebee visits a rose,
> As long as rosy infants are born
> No one believes it is happening now.

Only a white-haired old man, who would be a prophet
Yet is not a prophet, for he's much too busy,
Repeats while he binds his tomatoes:
There will be no other end of the world,
There will be no other end of the world.

A którzy czekali błyskawic i gromów, / Są zawiedzeni. / A którzy
czekali znaków i archanielskich trąb, / Nie wierzą, że staje się już. /
Dopóki słońce i księżyc są w górze, / Dopóki trzmiel nawiedza róże, /
Dopóki dzieci różowe się rodzą, / Nikt nie wierzy, że staje się
już. / / Tylko siwy staruszek, który byłby prorokiem, / Ale nie jest
prorokiem, bo ma inne zajęcie, / Powiada przewiązując pomidory: /
Innego końca świata nie będzie. / Innego końca świata nie będzie.

For Miłosz, apocalypse and normality had become one.

The arrival of peace brought no relief. Warsaw was in ruins,
the nation's population was decimated, and the future promised
only further political turmoil. It was impossible to return to
themes of prewar life; the world had ended and the dead de-
manded their due. The heavy burden borne by the survivors is
lamented in the poem "In Warsaw." Miłosz considers here the
new irony of his situation: he who had sworn he would not turn
his nation's wounds into objects of worship, after the manner of
the romantics, now was unable to tear himself away from contemplation of Poland's misery. Moved as he was by her suffering,
he rebelled nonetheless at being caught fast in the chains
of mourning:[11]

> I did not want to love like this,
> That was not my intention.
> I did not want to pity like this,
> That was not my intention.
> My pen is lighter
> Than a hummingbird's feather. This burden
> Is more than I can bear.
> How can I live in this land,
> Where my foot stumbles over
> The unburied bones of my loved ones?
> I hear voices; I see smiles. I can write
> Nothing, because five pairs of hands
> Clutch at my pen

And order me to write their stories,
The stories of their life and death.
Is this what I was created for—
To become a professional mourner?
I want to sing of festivities,
Of the joyous groves to which
Shakespeare has led me. Allow
Your poets a moment of joy
For your world is doomed to perish.

Nie chciałem kochać tak, / Nie było to moim zamiarem. / Nie chciałem litować się tak, / Nie było to moim zamiarem. / Moje pióro jest lżejsze / Niż pióro kolibra. To brzemię / Nie jest na moje siły. / Jakże mam mieszkać w tym kraju, / Gdzie noga potrąca o kości / Niepogrzebane najbliższych? / Słyszę głosy, widzę uśmiechy. Nie mogę / Nic napisać, bo pięcioro rąk / Chwyta mi moje pióro / I każe pisać ich dzieje, / Dzieje ich życia i śmierci. / Czyż na to jestem stworzony, / By zostać płaczką żałobną? / Ja chcę opiewać festyny, / Radosne gaje, do których / Wprowadził mnie Szekspir. Zostawcie / Poetom chwilę radości, / Bo zginie wasz świat.

The chains of history, as Miłosz quickly learned, lay in the future as well as the past. It would be many years before he would feel free to return in his poetry to that "first movement" of joyous singing.

IV   *Settling Accounts: Poetry of the Postwar Years*

Miłosz's first collection of postwar poems, *Światło dzienne* (Daylight), published in France in 1953, is concerned almost exclusively with reflections on the nature of history and the fate of poetry in Poland. *Daylight* can be read as the record of an inner crisis during which Miłosz attempted to balance the competing demands of loyalty to country, social ties, personal comfort, his sense of moral integrity, and his need as a poet for freedom to write and an audience to address. Miłosz's bleak outlook during this period of self-confrontation is most fully expressed in the lengthy poem, "A Moral Treatise," which provides a somber discussion of a serious ethical dilemma: To what extent should the individual allow himself to be bound by history and society?

A disarmingly simple form—rhymed couplets of traditional brief,
eight-syllable lines—crisply emphasizes the intellectual vigor of
Miłosz's argumentation. The poet admits that there are no final
answers. All he can do is issue a warning based on common
sense: be wary of all theories that pretend to predict the future
or define the essence of humanity. He admits that he cherishes no
illusions about a miraculous spring succeeding the winter darkness, and yet he nourishes the frail hope that something can
yet be done about man's endless suffering:[12]

> We have seen too many crimes
> To be able to renounce the good
> And sit down peacefully to breakfast
> Saying, "Blood is cheap today";
> Or, acknowledging the inevitability of delirium,
> To accept it as our daily bread.
> And so remember—in a time of troubles
> You must be an ambassador of dreams.

Zbyt wieleśmy widzieli zbrodni / Byśmy się dobra wyrzec mogli / I
mówiąc: krew jest dzisiaj tania—/ Zasiąść spokojnie do śniadania, /
Albo konieczność widząc bredni / Uznawać ją za chleb powszedni. /
A więc pamiętaj—w trudną porę, / Marzeń masz być ambasadorem.

Miłosz was far too skeptical a thinker, however, to be deluded
by the hope of acting as the rock which might deflect the lava
flow of totalitarianism (an image from "A Moral Treatise"). As
he well knew, any attempt at becoming an "ambassador of
dreams" carried with it the danger of joining the vast numbers
of moral schizophrenics whom he saw around him. He ended his
treatise on morality with a grim prophecy: "Before us lies the
heart of darkness" ("Przed nami jest—Jądro ciemności").

Although Stalinism may have represented the heart of darkness, Miłosz was not prepared to ally himself in thoughtless
reaction with the alternative schizophrenia which he perceived
in London's émigré circles. In one section of "Toast," a long
poem dedicated to his high school classmates, Miłosz bitterly
attacked those "romantics" in London who managed to find
something poetically heroic in the deaths of thousands of young
men during the doomed Warsaw Uprising of 1944.[13]

Not only London and Warsaw represented vile distortions of humane values; all of European civilization, as Miłosz perceived it at that time, was corrupt. Miłosz is at his most cynical in what is probably his best poem of this period—"Child of Europe". Adopting the coldly cynical posture of an initiate into the secrets of the century, Miłosz offers ironic instruction in the manners and morals of the age, justifying his presumption by the peculiar virtue of having survived:[14]

> Having the choice of our own death and that of a friend,
> We chose his, coldly thinking: let it be done quickly.
>
> . . . .
>
> As befits human beings, we explored good and evil.
> Our malignant wisdom has no like on this planet.
> Accept it as proved that we are better than they.
> The gullible, hot-blooded weaklings, careless with their
>   lives.

Do wyboru mając śmierć własną i śmierć przyjaciela / Wybieraliśmy jego śmierć, myśląc zimno: było się spełniło. / / . . . / / Jak należy się ludziom poznaliśmy dobro i zło. / Nasza złośliwa mądrość nie ma sobie równej na ziemi. / / Należy uznać za dowiedzione, że jesteśmy lepsi od tamtych, / Łatwowiernych, zapalnych a słabych, mało sobie ceniących życie.

In "Child of Europe" Miłosz drew no conclusions about the necessity of dreams, nor did he offer any hope of changing the course of history. Instead, he counseled a cultivated detachment as a protection from too bitter knowledge:

> Love no country: countries soon disappear.
> Love no city: cities are soon rubble.
>
> Throw away keepsakes, or from your desk
> A choking, poisonous fume will exude.
>
> Do not love people: people soon perish.
> Or they are wronged and call for your help.
>
> Do not gaze into the pools of the past.

Their corroded surface will mirror
A face different from the one you expected.

Nie kochaj żadnego kraju: kraje łatwo giną. / Nie kochaj żadnego
miasta: łatwo rozpada się w gruz. / / Nie przechowaj pamiątek, bo z
twojej szuflady / Wzbije się dym trujący dla twego oddechu. / / Nie
miej czułości dla ludzi: ludzie łatwo giną / Albo są pokrzywdzeni i
wzywają twojej pomocy. / / Nie patrz w jeziora przeszłości; tafla ich
rdzą powleczona / Inną ukaże twarz niż się spodziewałeś.

The cynicism expressed in "Child of Europe" displays, as in
the glare of a spotlight, the poet's lacerated consciousness.

Although the best of the poems in *Daylight* are proof that
political poetry can meet the dual standards of artistic excellence
and intellectual clarity (thus serving as models for the poet's
belief that art must be concerned with great ideas), Miłosz
turned to prose for a more fully reasoned statement of the intellectual costs of Communist political control. *The Captive Mind*
studies the reactions of four quite different writers to the lure of
belonging to history's vanguard, and is also an implicit intellectual autobiography. The extensive analysis to which he subjected the blandishments of historical materialism in *The Captive
Mind* brought to an end the most bitter and haunted period of
Miłosz's career.[15]

V *The Poetry of Exile*

A poet who chooses exile places himself in the lamentable
position of one who has lost both his ties with his native land
and his natural audience. Precisely because of these losses,
however, exile may be a liberating experience. Coupled with the
discovery of a new culture, these deprivations may encourage
the writer to experiment with form and to explore new themes.
Miłosz's work in exile during the past two and a half decades
has reflected both the personal pain and the liberating force of
his situation.[16] The frustration felt by most writers at the
inadequacy of language to express the particularity of experience
has been compounded in Miłosz's case by the fear that he is
writing into a void:[17]

So sensitive to the smells of hospitals and barracks, to the irrevocability of humiliation,

That I should have spent my life in a cork-padded cell, grinding my teeth,

I inherited gravity and stubbornness from some unknown ancestors and so I found a means:

The rhythmic rocking of patterned words, repeated on the street, in a bus, in bars, on roads,

And even more often in the half-sleep of early morning hours when consciousness surfaces like a devil's mountain.

But I was able to do this only in Polish, in a language which no one understands, except perhaps some hardheaded players in a Wabash or Milwaukee stadium.

And were I able not to speak, I would say nothing, because I am not indifferent to the fact that I am addressing no one.

Tak wrażliwy na zapach szpitali i koszar, na nieodwołalność poniżenia, / / Że powinien bym był spędzić życie w korkowej celi, szczękając zębami, / / Od nieznajomych przodków dostałem rozwagę i upór, więc wynalazłem sposób: / Rytmiczne kołysanie słów układanych, powtarzanych na ulicy, w autobusie, w barach, na drogach, / / a tym bardziej w półśnie rannych godzin, kiedy świadomość wynurza się jak diabelska góra. / / Ale umiałem to robić tylko po polsku, w języku który nikt nie rozumie, chyba twardogłowi zawodowcy stadionu w Wabash albo Milwaukee. / / I gdybym mógł nie mówić, nie mówiłbym nic, bo nie było mi obojętnie, że zwracam się do nikogo.

The suspicion that the poet is addressing no one has its advantages too. In his poetry published since *Daylight*—most notably in *Gucio zaczarowany* (literally, "Enchanted Gucio," but translated by Miłosz as "Bobo's Metamorphosis," 1965) and *Miasto bez imienia* (The City Without a Name, 1965)—Miłosz has been freer in experimenting with verse form. He has moved away from both the constraints of rhyme and the syllabic line of traditional Polish versification to which he adhered, as a rule, in his pre-exile work, and has adopted a relaxed free-verse style which at times verges on prose. Indeed, the title section of his latest collection, *Gdzie wschodzi słońce i kędy zapada* (Where the Sun Rises and Where It Sets, 1974), is a free mixture of verse and prose passages.

In his earliest prewar works, Miłosz's poetry displayed something of the overwritten quality of symbolist verse. In certain poems striking images followed each other in quick and startling succession.[18] Other poems already displayed the somber discursive mode which became the distinguishing characteristic of Miłosz's mature poetry. The "typical" Miłosz poem from the 1940s and 1950s adheres (in a relaxed modern fashion) to such traditional prosodic strictures as regulated line length, rhyme (even if approximate), stanzaic structure. Images are rare and are more likely to be metonymic than metaphoric. Emphasis is always placed on the theme or message which the neat form and the sonorous lines enhance.

The poems from the American period are marked by a decided relaxation of formal constraints. In a given poem lines may be of any length, conforming more to the natural rhythms of discourse than the prescribed rhythms of prosody. Rhyme is basically dispensed with. The mode is still discursive, but the tone is quieter, more contemplative than the assertive argumentation of, especially, the political works from the 1950s.

This loosening of formal constraints in the poetry parallels the introduction of new themes. The bitterly ironic perspective of the observer of historical process has yielded to a more meditative posture as Miłosz ponders the eternal philosophical questions of the nature of good and evil, of man's moral responsibility in a universe which often appears to be the plaything of demonic forces. A new sense of personal guilt becomes apparent in this period. In "To Raja Rao"—an unusual work in that it was written in English—Miłosz speaks of how he has turned away from the search for a just society to a confrontation with individual responsibility and individual guilt (which he labels Original Sin). Here we have Miłosz, the Eastern European intellectual, representative of a generation schooled in profound evil, drawing on his experience to counter the easy hopes now being proffered the next generation in his adopted America:[19]

> Link, if you wish, my peculiar case
> on the border of schizophrenia
> to the messianic hope
> of my civilization.
>
> Ill at ease in the tyranny, ill at ease in the republic,
> in the one I longed for freedom, in the other for the
>   end of corruption.
>
> Building in my mind a permanent *polis*
> for ever deprived of unnecessary bustle.
> . . . .
>
> I hear you saying that liberation is possible
> and that Socratic wisdom
> is identical with your guru's.
>
> No, Raja, I must start with what I am.
> I am those monsters which visit my dreams
> and reveal to me my hidden essence.
>
> If I am sick, there is no proof whatsoever
> that man is a healthy creature.
> . . . .
>
> No help, Raja, my part is agony,
> struggle, abjection, self-love and self-hate,
> prayer for the Kingdom
> and reading Pascal.

Although "To Raja Rao" is a relatively late work, it is characteristic of the metaphysical pessimism which is dominant in Miłosz's poetry of the late fifties and, again, of the late sixties and early seventies. A contrasting mood of joyful affirmation of the fullness of life appeared briefly during the early and mid-1960s. A quiet happiness, occasionally a joy which verges on ecstasy, shines through those poems in which Miłosz describes his discovery of what remains of the American wilderness. This

sudden emotional openness may well reveal the influence of
the short-lived California flower-children culture of the last
decade.

During the first years of exile, in the mid-1950s, Miłosz turned
to prose as well as to poetry in his search for a definition of
his personal-historical identity. In both the autobiographical
Native Realm and the exquisite novel of a Lithuanian boyhood,
Valley of the Issa—with its haunting evocation of demonic
forces which lurk barely concealed within a lyrically depicted
landscape—Miłosz tried to come to terms with the elusive past.

The autobiographical impulse is also present in the poetry of
this period, where it is often expressed through a dreamlike
perception of past and present dissolved in each other. The
exploration of memory and the subconscious through dream
imagery in such poems as "Album of Dreams" or "The City
Without a Name" is another new feature which distinguishes
the postexile poetry from Miłosz's earlier work. A recurrent
theme in these poems which look inward and backward is the
insistent approach of death. In "Rivers Grow Small," for example,
Miłosz muses on our changed perception of the past as life
approaches its conclusion. In the forceful final line of the poem,
which suddenly raises an argument implicit in Miłosz's philosophy (a typical device in his poetry), he bluntly asserts that the
real problem in aging is the necessity of confronting one's human
limitations:[20]

> Rivers grow small. Cities grow small. And splendid gardens
>   show what we did not see there before: the crippled
>   leaves and dust.
>
>   .   .   .   .   .
> The features of my face melt like a wax doll in the fire.
> And who can consent at the mirror to a mere face of a man?

Rzeki maleją. Miasta maleją. Śliczne ogrody / Pokazują czego nie
widzieliśmy dawniej, kalekie liście i kurz. / . . . / Rysy twarzy top-
nieją jak na woskowej kukle zanurzonej w ogniu. / A kto zgodzi się
mieć w lustrze tylko twarz człowieka?

This same sense of metaphysical bewilderment can be portrayed lightly, even whimsically:[21]

> If I had to tell what the world is for me
> I would take a hamster or a hedgehog or a mole
> and place him in a theater seat one evening
> and, bringing my ear close to his humid snout,
> would listen to what he says about the spotlights,
> sounds of the music, and movements of the dance.

Gdybym miał przedstawić czym jest dla mnie świat / wziąłbym chomika albo jeża albo kreta, / posadziłbym go na fotelu wieczorem w teatrze / a przytykając ucho do mokrego pyszczka / słuchałbym co mówi o świetle reflektorów, / o dzwiękach muzyki i ruchach baletu.

Moments of pure joy, unsullied by lurking thoughts of death and life's senselessness, are very rare in Miłosz's opus. An unusual note of sheer exultation is elicited by the splendor of the California beaches and forests in "The Year":[22]

> I would have related, had I known how, everything
>   which a single memory can gather for the
>   praise of men.
> O sun, o stars, I was saying, holy, holy, holy, is our
>   being beneath heaven and the day and our
>   endless communion.

Opowiadałbym gdybym umiał wszystko co jedna pamięć może zebrać na chwałę ludzi. / O słońce, o gwiazdy, mówiłem, święty, święty, święty, byt nasz podniebny i dzień i wieczne obcowanie.

The ecstasy of "The Year" is so unexpected as to strike an almost discordant note. More typical of Miłosz's poems of affirmation is "The Gift," from his latest verse collection *Where The Sun Rises . . . :*[23]

> A day so happy.
> Fog lifted early, I worked in the garden.
> Hummingbirds were stopping over honeysuckle flowers.
> There was no thing on earth I wanted to possess,
> I knew no one worth my envying him.
> Whatever evil I had suffered, I forgot.
> To think that once I was the same man did not embarrass me.
> In my body I felt no pain.
> When straightening up, I saw the blue sea and sails.

Dzień taki szczęśliwy. / Mgła odpadła wcześnie, pracowałem w ogrodzie. / Kolibry przystawały nad kwiatem kaprifolium. / Nie było na ziemi rzeczy, którą chciałbym mieć. / Nie znałem nikogo, komu warto byłoby zazdrościć. / Co przydarzyło się złego, zapomniałem. / Nie wstydziłem się myśleć, że byłem kim jestem. / Nie czułem w ciele żadnego bólu. / Prostując się, widziałem niebieskie morze i żagle.

Such moments of quiet pleasure in nature's beauty and acceptance of self are by no means the product of a sentimental belief in natural harmony or a belated, uncritical acceptance of the world as it is. Even the tributes to beauty arise from Miłosz's constant awareness that not civilization alone, but the natural order, too, is based on endless cruelty and violence. In section 7 of "Throughout Our Lands," for example, Miłosz describes a lovely May day in California, only to discern beneath its apparent harmony the realm of hideous spirits:[24]

> Only this is worthy of praise. Only this: the day.
> But beneath it elemental powers are turning somersaults:
> and devils, mocking the naive who believe in them,
> play catch with hunks of bloody meat,
> whistle songs about matter without beginning or end,
> and about the moment of agony
> when everything we have cherished will appear
> an artifice of cunning self-love.

Tylko to. Tylko to godne jest opiewania: dzień. / / Ale pod nim koziołkują moce elementarne / i diabły wykpiwające naiwnych co wierzą w ich istnienie / przerzucają się zwałami krwawego mięsa, / gwiżdżą pieśni o materii bez początku ni celu / i o chwili naszej agonii, / kiedy postępem cwanej miłości własnej / wyda się wszystko co kochaliśmy.

Precisely the precariousness of beauty in our world of violence renders it precious. This conviction is implicit in much of Miłosz's poetry of the past decade or so. It is stated explicitly in the poem "Counsels," where Miłosz offers his advice to the young poets of today. Acknowledging that he has lived through times when "Man has been given to understand / that he lives only by the grace of those in power," Miłosz explains that this experience has shown him the value of uncommitted poetry. Despite his lifelong dedication to poetry as a medium for intellectual expression, he concludes his words of advice with a delicate, elliptical defense of the celebration of beauty in poetry, resolving for himself the conflict he had experienced during the war when duty and poetry seemed to present irreconcilable demands:[25]

> There is so very much death, and that is why affection
> for pigtails, bright-colored skirts in the wind,
> for paper boats no more durable than we are. . . .

Jest bardzo dużo śmierci i dlatego tkliwość / dla warkoczy, spodnic kolorowych na wietrze, / łódeczek papierowych nie trwalszych niż my sami. . . .

VI *Conclusion*

The decision to go into exile marked a significant turning point in Miłosz's poetic development. Miłosz's exile poems are both more intimate than his earlier works and, at the same time, more universal. Miłosz remains an intellectual poet who uses the expressiveness of verse form to give voice to his philosophical concerns. He relies only rarely on the musical possibilities of versification (although his controlled lines often attain a stunning resonance) and uses metaphor and symbolic imagery with great restraint. To quote the eminent critic Zbigniew Folejewski, his is "a matter-of-fact poetry, filtered through philosophical reflections, exotic in personal retrospective detail, and universally valid in its awareness of modern man's problems."[26]

In America, as in his native Poland, Miłosz has refused to relinquish the role of citizen which he considers to be one of the poet's most important roles. He has continued to explore questions of historical development, the place of culture in contemporary civilization, and the meaning of individual guilt and responsibility in both his poetry and his essays, although the emphasis of his concern has shifted over the years from the more narrowly political to the more broadly philosophical. Thus, Miłosz has aligned himself with a tradition which goes back in Poland to the great romantic poets of the nineteenth century. Although Miłosz shares the romantics' sense of the poet's duty, he does not share their sense of divine mission. When Miłosz hears the voices of angels summoning him, the duty they impose on him as a poet is no different from that imposed on every man:[27] "day draws near / another one / do what you can" ("zaraz dzień / jeszcze jeden /zrób co możesz").

The aim of Miłosz's poetry has been the exploration of man's moral predicament in an often diabolical universe. From a position of profound skepticism, tempered by an abiding delight in beauty, Miłosz is constantly testing the limits both of faith and of despair.

CHAPTER 4

Tadeusz Gajcy and Krzysztof Kamil Baczyński: History's Victims

P RZYBOŚ and Miłosz belonged to a generation of writers who were already experienced artists when the catastrophic events anticipated by them erupted on September 1, 1939. During the succeeding five and a half years of war and occupation, a new generation of writers came to maturity under conditions of extraordinary hardship. These young men and women, born during the early 1920s, belonged to the first generation of Poles in well over a century who had begun life in an independent nation. Their childhoods coincided with the years of Poland's great postindependence euphoria; their adolescence, in contrast, was framed in a decade of growing anxiety as the shaky international economic and political situation cast its ominous shadow upon the newly independent nation. On the brink of adulthood, this ill-fated generation was plunged by historical events into a world of barbaric cruelty.

In succeeding chapters we shall turn our attention to a number of poets of the generation of the twenties who survived the war and went on to become leading figures in Poland's postwar literary renaissance. But first we must consider the meteoric careers of two remarkable poets of this generation—Tadeusz Gajcy and Krzysztof Kamil Baczyński—both of whom died during the Warsaw Uprising of 1944.

I Biographical Notes

Tadeusz Gajcy was born in Warsaw in 1922, the son of a railroad mechanic and a midwife. He was in the last year of his Catholic-school education when the war began. Gajcy fought as

a volunteer in the doomed defense of Warsaw in September,
1939—a searing experience which returns as a haunting motif in
his poetry. After the defeat of Poland Gajcy and his family settled
down to the difficult job of surviving. In 1941 he enrolled in the
Polonistics department of the underground Warsaw University,
where he met other aspiring young authors. Though he had tried
his hand at poetry and poetic prose as early as 1939, the first
works which he intended for eventual publication date from the
war period.

Publication under wartime circumstances was not the routine
joint venture between business and the creative artist that it is
in normal times. Under the stringent rules promulgated by the
Nazi occupation, publication in Polish of any but officially cleared
informational materials was strictly prohibited. Publishing became a conspiratorial activity undertaken at enormous risk to
everyone involved in it. Works were almost always printed in
mimeographed or crudely typeset form under pseudonyms; dis-
tribution was accomplished through a network of friends and
couriers who saw in the struggle to disseminate the written word
an act of heroism equivalent to guerrilla action—as, indeed,
it was.

Gajcy's first published volume, *Widma* (Specters), consisting
of the long title poem plus seven shorter works, was issued in
May, 1943, in a relatively large run of 250 copies. Gajcy used the
pseudonym Karol Topornicki; he was to use part of this name,
Topór (The Ax), as his *nom de guerre* when he enrolled in the
Home Army guerrilla units in defense of Warsaw in 1944. In
the spring of 1944 a second volume of "Topornicki's" poetry,
Grom powszedni (Our Daily Thunder), was published in an
edition of 500 copies. Most of Gajcy's work, however, was published posthumously.

Even in the fragmented life of the occupied capital there were
coherent literary groupings and cultural coteries. Gajcy was
associated with a group of writers whose literary focus was their
underground monthly journal, *Sztuka i Naród* (*Art and the
Nation*), of which he eventually became the fourth and last
editor. Each of the four editors' terms in office was terminated
by death.

From early 1943 until his death in the summer of 1944 Gajcy

was also involved in various underground activities in addition to the secret university. In May of 1943 he and two friends decided upon a noble if foolhardy gesture: on the occasion of Copernicus's birthday they attempted to lay a red-and-white wreath (Poland's national colors) at the base of the memorial statue to the great astronomer whom the Poles and the Germans both claimed as "their own." In an exchange of gunfire, possibly initiated by Gajcy in a moment of panic, one of his friends was killed. Gajcy escaped, but the experience is said to have marked him with an indelible sense of guilt—a belief that he would have to expiate this sin with his own early death. When the Warsaw Uprising broke out, Gajcy joined a partisan detachment assigned to the defense of the Old City. He died there when the Germans dynamited his headquarters building on August 16. His body was exhumed and buried in July, 1945.[1]

The broad outlines of the life of Krzysztof Baczyński are similar to Gajcy's. He, too, was born in Warsaw—in 1921. Baczyński, however, was born into an intellectual milieu. His father was a literary critic whose political leanings were toward a loosely defined Marxism. His mother, a writer of children's stories, was a worshipper of poetry who nurtured the promise of genius in her only child. Baczyński's first poetic efforts date from as early as 1936; his first political activity, membership in the joint socialist-communist Spartacus League, also dates from his high school years.

By early 1940 Baczyński was already known to established older writers (among them Jerzy Andrzejewski and Jarosław Iwaszkiewicz), but he remained aloof from their proffered benevolence. Baczyński's first publication was a typescript of seven poems which was distributed in the summer of 1940. His first book, *Wiersze wybrane* (Selected Poems), appeared in the autumn of 1942 in a mimeographed edition of ninety-six copies issued under the pseudonym, Jan Bugaj. It drew the immediate favorable attention of older writers, chief among them the critic Kazimierz Wyka.[2] One year later, Baczyński published his *Arkusz poetycki Jana Bugaja* (Jan Bugaj's Poetic Sheet). Baczyński's work, like Gajcy's, was printed in full only posthumously.

In the summer of 1942 Baczyński enrolled in the underground

university's Polonistics department. He dropped out one year
later in order to concentrate on his poetry and his conspiratorial
work in the underground Home Army. In the summer of 1943
he enrolled as a cadet in the Home Army's officer training school
and although, as we shall see, he had serious doubts about the
ultimate rationality of Home Army policy, he remained faithful
to his ideal of loyalty to the nation until his untimely death during the Warsaw Uprising. Baczyński was killed by a German
sharpshooter on August 4, 1944, while on duty with his military
unit. His body was exhumed in 1947 and buried beside that of
his wife, Barbara, who succumbed from shrapnel wounds a few
weeks after her husband's death.[3]

II *Revival of Romantic Myths*

It was only natural that the poets who found themselves
trapped by the German occupation (like their contemporaries
who went into emigration) should look back to Poland's romantic
era of the mid-nineteenth century. After the successive partitions
of Poland, and particularly after the November Insurrection of
1830, literature had been one of the strongest bonds holding
the nation together and poets, particularly the "three bards"—
(Adam Mickiewicz, Juliusz Słowacki, and Zygmunt Krasiński)—
had stepped forward as moral spokesmen for their nation. The
myths generated during the romantic period have been extraor-
dinarily influential in Polish culture, serving as a tradition which
could be emulated or rebelled against, but which has had to be
taken seriously. Almost every Polish writer during World War II
felt compelled to define his position in relation to these myths.
    The question of the romantic heritage is a complex one, but the
central traditions about Polish poetry and history which it en-
shrines are clear: the poet is a seer who addresses his nation's
deepest spiritual needs and yearnings; he should, ideally, be a
soldier-poet, engaged in the nation's struggle for freedom; suffering can be redemptive; Poland, in particular, is the Christ
among nations suffering for the sins of mankind and will be re-
born after her many agonies. These mystical ideas were often expressed in a visionary poetry rich in imagery and unconcerned

with the "realistic" evocation of the events of the here and now.

The romantic legacy played an important role in the works of both Gajcy and Baczyński. In particular, each of them was clearly influenced by Juliusz Słowacki, though in different ways. Gajcy reveals this influence most strikingly in the dreamlike quality and the daring, almost baroque abundance of imagery in much of his work. Toward the most important, some would say pernicious, of the myths—the redemptive value of suffering—his attitude is ambivalent. He seems to have accepted it as a personal truth but rejected its validity for the nation as a whole. Baczyński's narrative poems, with their attempts at creating mythical settings in which heroic men are faced with the choice between personal happiness and sacrifice to the nation, also testify in form and theme to a romantic influence.

The romantic poets who created the ideal of the poet-soldier-seer lived in the relatively easy situation of exile. The myth of the poet-hero served them as balm for the guilt feelings generated by not having experienced the trials of actual combat. For their spiritual heirs in the mid-twentieth century, living by the inherited myth meant risking death. Both Gajcy and Baczyński considered that their poet's calling imposed a duty to bear arms and each of them, as we have seen, died in battle. The constant expectation of an early death pervades the poetry of both men and is one of the sources of its intensity.

III *Tadeusz Gajcy's World of Shadows*

The most striking aspect of Gajcy's poetry is the density of its imagery. A typical Gajcy poem is not a logical argument illustrated by a set of colorful images which lend it its "poetic" quality, but is, rather, the sum of a swarm of images whose interconnection, indeed, whose very meaning may not be clear when an attempt is made to analyze the work into its component parts. Hence, it is difficult to find appropriate excerpts to illustrate the quality of Gajcy's poetry. One needs to cite his long works in their entirety, but this cannot be done in a brief chapter. Among the numerous images which he uses, Gajcy particularly favors those based on fire, smoke, and ominous shadows. There is also much religious imagery which is not tied to any specific religious message but which adds to the somber tonality of the whole.

The ominous weight with which much of Gajcy's poetry is burdened can be felt in the opening lines of his characteristically titled long poem, "Specters":[4]

> Do you know that land beneath the icicles of blackened
>   flaming Candlemas tapers
> which formerly creaked with resin but creaks today
>   with membranes
> of huge bats' wings?
> Do you know that land
> where along paths of sighs
> float dead
> charred flowers and the bones of meadow and forest
>   beasts?

Czy znasz ten kraj pod soplami sczerniałych gorących **gromnic** / skrzypiący dawniej żywicą—dzisiaj błonami skrzydeł / nietoperzy ogromnych. / Czy znasz ten kraj, gdzie ścieżkami westchnień / płyną nieżywe / kwiaty zwęglone i kości zwierząt łąkowych i leśnych.

Because of its baroque indulgence in oxymoron (icicles of flaming candles; creaking of membranes and resin) and deliberately unclear syntax (is it "wings of huge bats" or "huge wings of bats"?) it is difficult to say what, precisely, each fragment of this excerpt means. The horrific effect of the whole, however, is clear enough. It stands as a terrifying introduction to Gajcy's nightmare vision of a world which has become a living hell.

Although Gajcy creates his poetic world out of fantastic imagery his poetry is not disengaged from the world of reality. The "real" world, which can be said to exist in his poems in two opposing incarnations—the idyllic land of peace and the hellish land of war—is also painfully present in his work. Indeed, Gajcy's striving toward a mystical, elusive world of metaphor which lies beyond "reality" reflects an urgent desire to find a sanctuary for poetry in a land which has suddenly been hurled from peace to war.

Gajcy's most interesting and successful works are his two long

poems—the above-mentioned "Specters" and a work which strad-
dles the boundary between narrative and drama, "Sunday Mystery Play."[5] "Specters" is composed of ten sections, which are
more like the fragments of a poetic cycle than the carefully
linked stages of a well-developed narrative poem. The repeated
question, "Do you know that land?" ("Czy znasz ten kraj"), which
appears in several parts of the work, stresses the poet's disorientation in the new world of apocalypse. The specters of the title
are the poet's mystical visions. He sees himself as the object of
a struggle between Satan and the forces of good.

After the opening depiction (cited above) of a land which
has been turned into a circle of hell, the poet foresees his own
death and afterlife. His fevered imagination grossly distorts the
traditional comforts offered by the church. In one of the visions,
for example, he sees a bishop singing the litany, but the pro-
cession behind the bishop includes pet hyenas and tortoises, and
the bishop's ring "gurgles blood." A menacing refrain echoes
through this section as the poet, in his dream, confronts the consequences of his own lack of faith: "Whosoever believes shall
survive, / but he who does not believe shall neither drink nor
eat" ("A przeżyje kto wierzy, / kto nie wierzy—nie wypije i nie
zje").

An occasional blissful dream replaces the horrendous visions
which predominate in the poem. At one point, his mother's shade
appears to the poet and begs him to retain his faith despite God's
apparent desertion:

> Love the fire which levels
> and incinerates your land like a wooden bridge;
> thus was born a solemn and courageous
> hero.
> Love the shell of unkind ore
> when it flies directly over your head,
> it has taught more than one man
> the meaning of love.

Kochaj płomień, który niweczy / i twą ziemią przepala jak kładkę / tak
się zrodził pochmurny i męski / bohater. / / Kochaj pocisk z niedob-
rego kruszcu, / gdy nad włosem ci leci prosty; / niejednego on przecież
nauczył / miłości.

The momentary hope of some good coming from the general
devastation is quickly dispelled, however. Gajcy describes the
arrival of spring, but the traditional symbolic meanings of the
season are reversed. Nature's fertility is an ominous warning
to man as grass destroys the asphalt in the streets, and the terrible rubble of the ruined city is bedecked with potato blossoms.
By the end of the poem it is clear that Satan will triumph over
both the poet and the city, and in a last frenzied outburst Gajcy
appeals to God for just a glimpse of His benevolence:

> Fish float on violet rivers, their bellies upturned,
> an old lady's last canary has breathed his death sigh,
> it used to be golden from his singing,
> now he lies there, his feathers stiff,
> so let us pray: deliver us from evil.
> The skin of the earth is wrinkling, caving in with
>   forests and bursting wide open,
> the stone heartrendingly sobs,
> a star is lost in the wind:
> the black sun has shrunk to the shape of a human heart
> so let us pray: be merciful,
> delay Thy ominous omen.
>
> . . . .
>
> The eyes of men are growing blind beneath the slashing
>   of a downy wing feather,
> not an olive branch from the sky stiff with frost,
> but like a drop from under Satan's fingernail
> falls an elongated bat.

Ryby na rzekach z fioletu wypływają brzuchami do góry, / ostatni
kanarek staruszki wydał śmiertelne westchnienie, / żółto było od śpie-
wu jego, / teraz leży—sztywne ma pióra—/ więc się módlmy: wybaw od
złego. / / Marszczy się skóra globu, lasami zapada i pęka, / płacze
serdecznie kamień, / gwiazda się traci na wietrze: / czarne słońce
zmalało do kształtu serca człowieka / więc się módlmy: daj zmił-
owanie, / oddal zapowiedź złowieszczą / / . . . / / Ślepną źrenice
ludzi pod cięciem puchowej lotki—/ nie gałązka oliwna z nieba ściętego
mrozem, / lecz podłużny opada jak kropla / spod paznokcia szatana—
nietoperz.

The blurred and sometimes confusing imagery of "Specters"

is an expressionistic dramatization of a spiritual crisis in one who yearns to be a believer but who sees in the monstrous events to which he is witness only two equally intolerable possibilities: either God does not exist or, if He does, then he has abandoned His world to evil. A similar unbearable doubt underlay the romantics' embracing of a mystical redemptive faith in the ultimate meaning of Poland's agony.

While "Specters" is a vivid dramatization of spiritual suffering, in "Sunday Mystery Play" Gajcy was able to step back from the romantic traditions which had enthralled him and, with searing irony, destroy the myths of the poet-prophet. In this long dramatic poem in four scenes and an intermezzo Gajcy deftly mocks the romantic tradition while using a poetic form derived directly from the romantics. The main characters in this tragifarce are Hipolit, a beggar-prophet who tries to convince the masses that apocalypse is imminent, and the Prophesying Cabby, who becomes a prophet in his own eyes because his horse is named Apocalypse. The drama is set in Warsaw on the eve of World War II, allowing Gajcy to exploit the absurd possibilities of a modern urban setting for a contemporary mystery play. The Prophesying Cabby, for example, is eager to win a prominent position on the political committee which undoubtedly will be established to deal with Apocalypse, and ominous fiery signs in the sky turn out to be an animated electric advertisement depicting an ever-pouring bottle of vermouth. The crowd is easily swayed, moving first to support Hipolit, then turning against him as soon as a usurper appears on the scene, and reverting to Hipolit once again when one of the signs of apocalypse which he has predicted comes true.

One can discern in "Sunday Mystery Play" reminiscences of each of the three Polish bards, along with a heavy admixture of satire and absurdity which marks this work as a particularly modern rejection of romantic hopes. The mystical prophecies recall Mickiewicz's fascination with the Cabala and mysticism, as well as Słowacki's late visionary works. The mockery of mysticism, on the other hand, is an echo of Słowacki's earlier attitude. And the derision of the mob as easy prey for demagogues, though it has roots outside Polish literature as well,

clearly repeats Krasiński's teachings in his *Nie-boska komedia*
(Undivine Comedy).

Despite this conscious rejection of the romantic myths Gajcy
maintained his fervent attachment to the national cause. He
continued to cling to his faith that his sacrifice for the nation
was meaningful and that his poetry would yet speak to a free
generation of Polish readers. In one of his last poems, "To My
Descendant," Gajcy described this faith, abandoning his usually
fevered metaphoric style in favor of an uncharacteristic straight-
forwardness:[6]

> And I know that bowing your troubled head
> over the furrow of letters you still see
> my image: I am walking through the air,
> and my city walks behind me.
>
> . . . .
> That time, that night and myself displaced
> weigh upon and teach you:
> the last dream, the first grief
> and a bitter love for one's fatherland.

I wiem, że chyląc głową trudną / nad liter bruzdą—widzisz jeszcze /
mój obraz: idę przez powietrze, / a za mną miasto moje idzie. / . . . /
Ten czas, ta noc i ja bez miejsca / nad tobą ważą się i uczą: / ostatni
sen, a boleść pierwsza / i słona miłość nad ojczyzną.

IV   Krzysztof Kamil Baczyński: Between Two Loves

In comparison with Gajcy's work, Krzysztof Baczyński's poetry
is luminous in its clarity and directness, although he too used
startling images and created his own myths. For convenience of
discussion Baczyński's poetry can be divided into three general
groupings: his love lyrics dedicated to his wife, Barbara; his
patriotic poems on the personal lessons he derived from the war
experience; and his longer narrative poems which include elements of both myth and epic. Baczyński's verse is permeated
with a longing for "pure" poetry, for the freedom to retreat into
the world of the imagination whose existence is its own justification. But reality and a sense of duty constantly deflect the
poet's attention from the realm of fantasy. While the poems to

Barbara are located more in the sphere of pure poetry and the patriotic poems in the sphere of duty, in the long narrative poems Baczyński attempted to reconcile the two opposing forces.

Baczyński's love poetry is extremely delicate. He makes frequent use of images which are pure, transparent, and fluid in order to evoke a blend of erotic and spiritual love. He surrounds Barbara with images of light and graceful movement: moonlight, snow, waterfalls, mirrors. She is a crystal vessel, a birch tree, a white wind whose purity is redemptive for the man who loves her. The subtlety with which Baczyński evokes the transformation of the corporeal into the spiritual is, perhaps, best demonstrated in one of his most beautiful love lyrics, "White Magic":[7]

> Standing before a mirror of silence,
> her hands in her hair, Barbara
> pours into her crystal body
> the silver drops of her voice.
>
> Then like a pitcher
> she is filled with light
> and crystalline she enfolds the stars
> and the white dust of the moon.
>
> Through the quivering prism of her body
> in the music of white sparks
> ermines will slink
> like fluffy leaves of sleep.
>
> Bright from the northern stars
> bears will be covered by frost
> and a stream of mice will cross
> flowing like a babbling avalanche.
>
> At last milkily replete
> she will slowly fall asleep
> and time will descend melodiously
> like a waterfall of light.
>
> Barbara's body is silver. Within,
> the white ermine of silence

softly arches its back
beneath an invisible hand.

Stojąc przed lustrem ciszy / Barbara z rękami u włosów / nalewa w
szklane ciało / srebrne kropelki głosu. / / I wtedy jak dzban–światłem / zapełnia się i szkląca / przejmuje w siebie gwiazdy / i
biały pył miesiąca. / / Przez ciała drżący pryzmat / w muzyce białych
iskier / łasice się prześlizną / jak snu puszyste listki. / / Oszronią się w
nim niedźwiedzie, / jasne od gwiazd polarnych, / a myszy się strumień
przewiedzie / płynąc lawiną gwarną. / / Aż napełniona mlecznie, /
w sen się powoli zapadnie, / a czas melodyjnie osiądzie / kaskadą
blasku na dnie. / / Więc ma Barbara srebrne / ciało. W nim pręży się
miękko / biała łasica milczenia / pod niewidzialną ręką.

The image of Barbara or the beloved woman appears not
only in such pure love lyrics as "White Magic" but also in the
short patriotic poems and the longer narrative poems. There
it functions as a reminder of the domestic tranquillity which
must fall victim to the harsh demands of duty. In "Two Loves"
Baczyński compares his love for a woman's frail body with
his fatal love for the land in which his brothers are turning to
ashes.[8] The terrible choice between two loves appears again and
again in Baczyński's poetry. It is present in veiled form beginning with his earliest wartime works and becomes more insistent
from 1943 on.

In the narrative poem, "The Glass Bird: A Fairy-Tale Poem,"
written in the autumn of 1941, Baczyński was already contemplating the choice that he knew would eventually confront him,
but his concern was disguised in a pseudomythical fantasy.[9] In
this twelve-part work Baczyński tells the story of a young hero
who sets off to unknown worlds in order to bring peace and
harmony to his troubled land. Miłun ("Man of Love"–the name
has a mythic resonance), like an epic hero who embodies the
life forces of earth, has roots in the land and arms that can
reach to the sky; his veins are filled with the trees' green blood
and he is mighty as a granite cliff. The land he loves is a place
of great beauty and abundance, the fields bursting with grain
and the forests as lovely as woven tapestries, but the close
observer can notice beneath the surface the graves of men and
the swelling tears of human misery.

In answer to a spiritual summons the intrepid Miłun bids farewell to his wife and sons and sets out across the menacing seas to seek the gift of happiness. He visits mountainous glaciers in whose glassy peaks the world of misery is mirrored. From there he descends to the depths of the sea which mirrors the glacial heights. At last, like every epic hero who sets out on such a quest, Miłun realizes that he must find his answer on earth.

On his way home Miłun is swept by the winds to a place of pure transparency where crystal people, moved by his words about the suffering in his native land, make him the gift of a glass bird which nests in a transparent tree. Miłun carries the bird to his homeland where a society of strangers has established itself in his absence. A chorus tells Miłun of the violence that has visited the land and warns him that he must understand and accept death. With the gift of life in his hand, Miłun rejects the gloomy teachings of the chorus. At that moment a giant peasant comes on the scene and with his crude mocking laughter shatters the glass bird.[10] Defeated, Miłun remains rooted like a mighty spruce in his land, blessing it with his broken heart and "green song."

Like the eponymous hero of the *Gilgamesh*, Miłun sets out on a quest whose ultimate purpose is to overcome death. But whereas Gilgamesh is concerned with personal immortality, this modern epic hero has a more communal goal: to bring happiness to the living and to protect them from death at the hands of violent marauders. In both cases, the quest leads only to the acquisition of bitter knowledge. The Babylonian hero glimpses the secret of eternal life but quickly loses it, just as Miłun, who holds the glass bird of happiness in his hands, is powerless to protect its fragile promise of tranquillity in a world overrun by men of violence.

Baczyński never lost sight of this tragic vision. His commitment to Poland's struggle and his insistence on joining the underground gains poignancy when one realizes that it was an allegiance unsupported by any belief in a future age of peace. Not only did he have his doubts about the ultimate triumph of Poland, but he also foresaw for every participant in the struggle a personal defeat that would be worse than death. For Baczyński, the acceptance of a soldier's duty carried a heavy penalty. The survivors of the fight for Poland's freedom, he believed, would emerge from the war morally deadened by the killing which they had undertaken as a moral obligation. In this assessment he was somewhat ahead of his time; the contamination of the survivors was to emerge as an important theme in postwar literature.[11]

Baczyński gave voice in a number of short poems to the pessimism which beset him. One of the most direct expressions of this mood is "Prayer II" in which the image of the crucified Christ is evoked to dramatize the sins of the victims:[12]

> Not one of us is without guilt. When night falls
> your faces and mine drip blood
> and one's own body is like a betrayal of the spirit,
> and hateful are the nails through one's own hands.

Nikt z nas nie jest bez winy. Kiedy noc opada, / wasze twarze i moja ociekają krwią / i własne ciało jest jak duszy zdrada, / i nienawistne ćwieki własnych rąk.

Baczyński's ambivalence about his political posture is clear. His poems which issued a direct call to arms were undoubtedly sincere. (One of the most famous of these vibrates with the fierce battle cry: "Oh, seize the sword of history and strike! and strike!")[13] The most poignant of his shorter poems on the theme of reconciling his vision, his poetic calling, and history's insistent summons, is "To My Parents." Taking stock of his parents' hopes for their child who was "like the linden tree's rustle," Baczyński attributes the split within his own soul to his father's and mother's differing expectations of how their son would carry on the struggle for freedom, his father stressing the masculine principle of active participation and his mother, the feminine principle of using words. Baczyński questions each of these expectations, underlining the enormous sacrifice that each demands:[14]

> Father, it's a hard life at war.
> .   .   .   .
> Why give such a faith to a child,
> why this inheritance like a house aflame?

Before twenty years pass
life will die for him in the daisies of his hands.

And what good is a thought like a pine tree,
its head too high when they chop down the trunk?
And how simple the path is
when the awkward heart is dust.

I cannot name things, mother, it's too painful,
death is striking too fiercely from every side.
Love, mother—I no longer know if it exists.
My distended nostrils sniff out God from afar.

. . . .

Day or night—mother, father—I shall stand my ground,
in the crashing of bullets, I, a soldier, a poet, the dust of time.
I shall go on . . . this I have from you: I do not fear death,
carrying onwards my bouquet of yearnings like charred roses.

Ojcze, na wojnie twardo / . . . / / I po cóż wiara taka dziecinie, / po
cóż dziedzictwo jak płomieni dom? / Zanim dwadzieścia lat minie, /
umrze mu życie w złocieniach rąk. / / A po cóż myśl taka jak sosna, /
za wysoko głowica, kiedy pień tną. / A droga jakże tak prosta, / gdy
serce niezdarne—proch. / / Nie umiem, matko, nazwać, nazbyt boli, /
nazbyt mocno śmierć uderza zewsząd. / Miłość, matko—już nie wiem,
czy jest. / Nozdrza rozdęte z daleka Boga wietrzą. / / . . . / / Dzień
czy noc—matko, ojcze—jeszcze ustoję / w trzaskawicach palb, ja, żołnierz, poeta, czasu kurz. / Pójdę dalej—to od was mam: śmierci się
nie boję, / dalej niosąc naręcza pragnień jak spalonych róż.

Baczyński's decisive word on the theme of duty to country
is his narrative poem, "The Choice."[15] Among his most famous
but not most successful works (it is in parts mawkish and overwritten), it confronts once more the opposition between personal, domestic love and a higher love whose price is death. In
this tale, the poet's alter ego is the artist Jan who leaves his
pregnant young wife, Maria, to defend his city and dies during
the street fighting. When an angel comes to claim Jan's soul
(this admission of the reader to the heavenly realms is a romantic
echo), Jan catches a glimpse through the clouds of Maria bent
over their newborn child. His spirit tries to struggle back to earth
to protect her, but the angel guides him ever upward, assuring

Jan that the purity of his choice and his love which encompassed more than Maria will provide the safeguard for the child that his presence on earth could not assure.

That Baczyński made himself act in conformity with such a faith is understandable. That he actually believed in the angel's promise is harder to accept, given the overwhelming evidence of the many troubled poems he wrote on this theme. Yet in the emotional criticism which comprises much that has been written in Poland about Baczyński, this poem is often cited as proof of the poet's moral steadfastness, as if a canonical work were absolutely necessary to shore up a monument to this martyred soldier-poet.

V   *Conclusion*

It is idle to speculate on how any writer might have developed had he been granted a longer life; yet when confronted with two such immensely talented poets as Gajcy and Baczyński, who met such tragically early deaths (at ages twenty-two and twenty-three, respectively), the temptation is irresistible. It appears that the war did not have as grossly distorting an impact on Gajcy's "natural" poetic style as it did on Baczyński's. Obviously, the nightmarish specters that haunt Gajcy's poetry are the products of his rude awakening to war from a quiet childhood. But the seeming ease with which he transformed them into the substance of poetry through the rich variety of his metaphors indicates that Gajcy was able to merge the content pressed upon him by his times with his own peculiar aesthetic sensibility. It can be assumed that had he lived Gajcy would have continued to explore, through fantastic metaphors which make the unreal contiguous with the real, the furthest reaches of the subconscious in its confrontation with reality.

Baczyński, on the other hand, appears to have suffered more from the split between the direction he desired for his poetry and the path which he felt compelled to follow. His earliest prewar poems dealt with exotic landscapes and marvelous creatures of land and sea.[16] His fantasy, when it was temporarily freed from the constraints of the historical moment, functioned most happily in a magical borderland where one form of life shades into another, or is transformed through metamorphosis. In the relatively early poem, "A Little Song," for example, in which the poet thinks of death not as nothingness (as he would within a few months) but as an escape back to the happiness of childhood, fear becomes "a white deer floating away on the butterfly dance of its legs" ("Upływa lęku biały jeleń / w motylim pląsie nóg").[17]

Such delicately fanciful imagery recurs in Baczyński's exquisite love poems and in his only lighthearted long work, "The Poet's Wedding," which offers a veritable feast of this type of description.[18] Issuing the ritual invitation to his bride to share his home, the poet describes his dwelling place in images and rhythms which echo the naiveté of folk poetry. These lines may be read not only as a charming description of the place where the poet of the poem dwelt, but also as a picture of his soul's abode, the world of fantasy for which Baczyński yearned:

> There it's always autumn,
> and a rosy lion
> gathers golden apples
> beneath the rows of trees.
> There it's always winter,
> and a deep blue moose
> spirits a branch of white dreams
> to the icy arch of the clouds.
> There it's always springtime,
> a verdant bird casts off
> wings of ruddy fire
> on the smoking green.
> There it's always summer,
> a golden bear averts
> his head, etched in honey,
> from the wrinkled streams.

Tam jest zawsze jesień, / pod krużgankiem drzew / zbiera złote jabłka / różowawy lew. / Tam jest zawsze zima, / w chmur lodowy luk / modry łoś unosi / gałąż białych snów. / Tam jest zawsze wiosna, / na dymiącą ruń / ptak zielony zrzuca / skrzydła rudych łun. / Tam jest zawsze lato, / od zmarszczonych rzek / żółty niedźwiedź zwraca / ryty w miodzie łeb.

Despite the indications that Baczyński would have wished to give himself up once more to the lure of pure poetry, it is by no means clear that such a return would have been possible for him. As we shall see in the following chapters, the experience of war and the guilty pain of survival were so devastating as to cast a pall over the poetic creation of the entire generation born in the 1920s and to virtually eliminate fantasy as a creative possibility. Stern, unadorned reality was to become the watchword of the day as a new sense of responsibility to the destroyed past succeeded the taskmaster of patriotic duty to whom Gajcy and Baczyński had each paid their dues.

CHAPTER 5

Tadeusz Różewicz: Poetry and Antipoetry

AMONG contemporary Polish poets, Tadeusz Różewicz is probably the most famous outside his native country. His international renown has been based in large measure on his widely translated dramatic works, but in Poland his name is almost synonymous with postwar poetry.[1] In the early postwar years Różewicz most forcefully expressed both the sense of moral dislocation experienced by the survivors and the writer's despair at ever finding again in his language untainted words and forms which could convey the new reality. Like Krzysztof Baczyński, his exact contemporary, Różewicz found himself assigned by history to the dual roles of victim and avenger. As a survivor of the carnage, he was left to confront the moral issues which Baczyński had foreseen before his death. The blood guilt which Baczyński so poignantly depicted is a central issue of Różewicz's poetry. His pained outrage at having been turned into an instrument of murder (in however just a cause) is compounded by the burden of finding himself unaccountably a survivor, torn, as survivors of great catastrophes often are, between the natural urge to live and enjoy life and the paralyzing summons of the dead.[2]

As noticed above, a similar conflict occurs in the early postwar poetry of Czesław Miłosz. Różewicz's pain is similar in many respects to Miłosz's but his poetic resolution of the conflict is different. While Miłosz was an accomplished poet and mature adult with a developed sense of self to rely on at the outbreak of the war, Różewicz had to forge for himself a new identity as man and poet and, simultaneously, a new poetic language. What resulted was a poetic form which critics have termed "antipoetry": a style stripped of traditional adornments and artifice, in which naked facts, deprived of the usual softening effects

73

74 CONTEMPORARY POLISH POETRY

of musicality, abstract imagery, or elevated language, launch a frontal attack on the reader's emotions. Subtlety is rejected in favor of extreme directness; the poet insists on confronting the ugliest of facts without any attempt at glossing over them. "I am twenty years old / I am a murderer," he declares bluntly in the early poem, "Lament,"[3] and this insistence on avoiding euphemisms becomes his hallmark.

Różewicz burst onto the literary scene as an outraged moralist, a young man who had witnessed the worst betrayal of Western civilization's moral premises and who felt it his mission to keep that betrayal in the forefront of his reader's consciousness. Like his contemporary, the prose writer Tadeusz Borowski,[4] Różewicz felt compelled to ward off heroic myths which might disguise the moral wilderness out of which the survivors had emerged. Like Borowski, he soon embraced Communism as a powerful antidote to the bourgeois values which had so cruelly betrayed his generation. But unlike Borowski, who, as it turned out, was only a temporary survivor (having escaped the ovens at Auschwitz, he took his own life by gas in 1951), Różewicz was not driven to the extreme of suicide. Having survived well beyond the immediate postwar period, he has had to shape his poetry to fit the demands of life as well as of the death from which he escaped. This process will be examined in the present chapter.

I Biographical Note

Tadeusz Różewicz was born in 1921 in the provincial town of Radomsko in central Poland, into a family of middle-class intelligentsia. His early life appears to have been uneventful; tragedy entered his world only with the advent of war. Różewicz's elder brother, a member of the underground, was executed by the Gestapo. Różewicz himself fought with the Home Army in 1943–1944.

Różewicz's earliest publications date from 1938, when some poems of his were printed in a student magazine. Under the pseudonym "Satyra" he also "published" one collection of prose and poetry, *Echa leśne* (Forest Echoes) toward the end of the war. After the war, Różewicz moved to Cracow where he began to study art history at the prestigious Jagiellonian University and to work seriously on his poetry. His first volume of poetry, *Niepokój* (Anxiety), which established his fame as a poet, was published in Cracow in 1945. From then until the late 1960s he published new collections of poetry at intervals of one or two years and, in addition, occasional volumes of short stories and plays.

In many respects a loner and an opponent of what he considers to be Poland's literary establishment, Różewicz dramatized his refusal to be co-opted into the world of literary awards and mutual admiration by his decision in 1949 to move from the cultural capital of Cracow to the grim industrial town of Gliwice in the mining area of the Upper Silesian basin. Though the move to Gliwice, may have been undertaken as a demonstration of his bona fides (this was the time when Różewicz's adherence to Communist doctrine was at its strongest), Różewicz remained for twenty years in what many another writer would consider cultural exile. During this time he continued writing without evident impediment, producing a sizable number of poems on the death of poetry, among other themes. Despite his frequently expressed fears of imminent world catastrophe, by marrying and raising a family he manifested a personal hope in the continuance of some sort of civilized existence.

Różewicz's isolation, however, was only apparent. He received early recognition as the spokesman for his generation and was permitted to publish with impressive frequency even during the Stalinist years. He has been awarded numerous literary prizes and has become one of the literary establishment's crowned antiestablishment figures. In this respect, his situation is akin to that of Julian Przyboś, with the important distinction that Różewicz has been more widely read and influential among his contemporaries than was the older poet. Since the late 1960s Różewicz has lived in Wrocław, also an industrial city, but one which is at the same time a center of cultural experimentation, particularly in theatrical art.

II *The Voice of His Generation*

Różewicz's reputation as the voice of his generation derives from his earliest collections of poetry, specifically the volumes

Anxiety and *Czerwona rękawiczka* (The Red Glove, 1948). In these two volumes the basic message is the impossibility of returning to "normal" life in its prewar form because of the haunting, paralyzing memory of one's dead comrades and one's own guilt. Thus, in "Lament" he defines himself as follows:[5]

> I am twenty years old
> I am a murderer
> I am an instrument
> as blind as the sword
> in the executioner's hand
> I murdered a man
> and with red fingers
> caressed the white breasts of women.

mam lat dwadzieścia / jestem mordercą / jestem narzędziem / tak ślepym jak miecz / w dłoni kata / zamordowałem człowieka / i czerwonymi palcami / gładziłem białe piersi kobiet.

Repeatedly in his early poetry Różewicz returns to this central image of the tainted survivor. In the famous poem, "The Survivor" (probably the most frequently anthologized of all his work), he utters a poignant cry for help, as moving as the dying Goethe's legendary demand for more light. Denying the validity of such concepts as love and hate, truth and falsehood, honor and transgression—ideas on which his generation was raised—the poet begs for the clarity which alone may make it possible for him to endure his survival:[6]

> I am seeking a teacher and a master
> let him return to me my sight hearing and speech
> let him once again name objects and concepts
> let him separate the light from the darkness.
>
> I am twenty-four years old
> led to the slaughter
> I survived.

Szukam nauczyciela i mistrza / niech przywróci mi wzrok słuch i mowę / niech jeszcze raz nazwie rzeczy i pojęcia / niech oddzieli światło od ciemności. / / Mam dwadzieścia cztery lata / ocalałem / prowadzony na rzeź.

Różewicz defines himself as a murderer groping for moral values in a destroyed civilization, a man whose spiritual suffering has led him to the one fundamental truth: twentieth-century man died a spiritual as well as a physical death during World War II. Despite his own sense of guilt, Różewicz's awareness of this fact compels him to stand in moral judgment over those who would ignore this central issue. Różewicz is absolutely certain of the extent of the surrounding darkness, but in the early poems he has very little sense of where the light he is seeking may be found. His poems, both early and late, radiate contempt for those who would too quickly seek solace from the past in the tawdry comforts of bourgeois existence or the oblivion of sex.[7] His moralizing, though it may become tiresome, is, however, rarely cheap, because it is as likely to be directed against himself as against others.

Self-contempt and revulsion against the pull toward life is accompanied in Różewicz's early poetry by a deep sense of loss. *Anxiety* and *The Red Glove* contain a number of extremely tender, even sentimental poems in which the poet grieves for the prewar past to which there is no return. The pain of his loss is compounded by the fact that he is mourning at once a lost world and the passing of his own childhood and youth. In "The Chestnut Tree," for example, he evokes a world of childhood which fits into the reduced dimensions of a doll house viewed through an autumnal haze: the mother is so tiny she should be carried rather than allowed to walk, soldiers are still just harmless little toys on a shelf, and God hangs limply powerless on the wall. In a melancholy mood the poet sums up the meaning of his youth: "Childhood is like an eroded face / on a gold coin which rings / pure" ("Dzieciństwo jest jak zatarte oblicze / na złotej monecie która dźwięczy / czysto").[8]

A similar lament for the irreversible separation of the survivor from his old world is expressed in "The Return":[9]

> Suddenly the window will open
> and mother will call me
> it's time to come home

the wall will part
and I shall enter heaven in my muddy boots

I'll sit at the table and churlishly
answer their questions

nothing's the matter leave
me alone. I'll just sit there
with my head in my hands. How can I
tell them about this long
and intricate road.

Here in heaven mothers
knit little green scarves
flies buzz

father nods by the stove
after six days of work.

No—I cannot tell them
that men jump
at other men's throats.

Nagle otworzy się okno / i matka mnie zawoła / już czas wracać / /
rozstąpi się ściana / wejdę do nieba w zabłoconych butach / / usiądę
przy stole i opryskliwie / będę opowiadał na pytania / / nic mi nie
jest dajcie / mi spokój. Z głową w dłoniach / tak siedzę i siedzę. / Jakże
im / opowiem o tej długiej / i splątanej drodze. / / Tu w niebie matki
robią / zielone szaliki na drutach / / brzęczą muchy / / ojciec drzemie
pod piecem / po sześciu dniach pracy. / / Nie—przecież nie mogę im /
powiedzieć / że człowiek człowiekowi / skacze do gardła.

   The one consistently gentle note in these early poems is the
theme of the innocence of the very young and the aged. Elderly
women represent for Różewicz the essence of love, endurance,
and undeserved suffering, while children elicit an almost maternal tenderness from this otherwise tough and cynical writer.
What children and old people appear to share is a touching
powerlessness which is especially attractive to Różewicz; these
members of the human race, at least, can be counted on to
remain among the victims, never among the victimizers. Róże-

wicz does not see in children the incarnation of humanity's hope for a better future; it can be deduced from his silence on this score that their state of powerless innocence is merely a temporary reprieve from human failings.

III *Escape Into the Future*

There was, however, one brief period in Różewicz's career when he did indulge in fantasies about a future world order of peace and harmony. During the worst of the Stalinist years, from approximately 1948 through 1952, Różewicz wrote poetry which suited the political demands of the period. In these, his weakest poems, collected in the volumes *Pięć poematów* (Five Narrative Poems, 1950), *Czas który idzie* (The Coming Age, 1951), *Wiersze i obrazy* (Poems and Images, 1952), and *Uśmiechy* (Smiles, 1955), there are two dominant themes. The first is a fear, no doubt genuine, of renewed warfare and eventual nuclear holocaust. This terror of another world war becomes especially strong after the outbreak of the Korean War. Although a revulsion against war is a logical extension of Polish experience, the political slanting of Różewicz's poems from this period is not. They are pieces of simplistic Stalinist propaganda in which all brutality in the world is attributed to capitalists and imperialists.[10] These poems are counterbalanced by the positive theme of the eventual triumph of socialism and its humanizing effect on mankind. In the title poem of *The Coming Age* Różewicz disavows as too negative his former preoccupation with death (for which he had been publicly criticized) and argues that salvation can be found only by joining the collective and embracing a communist faith:[11]

> The coming age is most beautiful
> people will not die like larvae
> communism will elevate men
> cleanse them of the age of contempt.

Czas który idzie jest piękniejszy / ludzie nie będą umierali jak larwy / komunizm ludzi podniesie / obmyje z czasów pogardy.

It is impossible to know to what extent these poems reflect

a genuine reversal in Różewicz's outlook and to what extent they represent a bowing to political pressure. One may assume, however, that a certain amount of censorship was involved (whether self-imposed or otherwise) because by the mid-1950s the old themes of the terrible tension between the pull to life and the chilling memory of the dead had resurfaced in Różewicz's poetry, never again to disappear entirely. Once more, Różewicz spoke as a survivor, claiming that he represented his emotionally crippled generation. In "Leave Us Alone" he harks back to the early theme of his generation as a collectivity of lost souls:[12]

> Forget about us
> about our generation
> live like human beings
> forget about us
>
> we envied
> plants and rocks
> we envied dogs
>
> I'd like to be a rat
> I said to her then
>
> I'd like not to be
> I'd like to fall asleep
> and wake up after the war
> she said with closed eyes
>
> forget about us
> don't ask about our youth
> leave us alone

zapomnijcie o nas / o naszym pokoleniu / żyjcie jak ludzie / zapomnijcie o nas / / my zazdrościliśmy / roślinom i kamieniom / zazdrościliśmy psom / / chciałbym być szczurem / mówiłem wtedy do niej / / chciałabym nie być / chciałabym zasnąć / a zbudzić się po wojnie / mówiła z zamkniętymi oczami / / zapomnijice o nas / nie pytajcie o naszą młodość / zostawcie nas.

In a related poem which follows closely upon this one, Różewicz returns to the vexing problem which he had evaded during

his years of simplistic Stalinism: how can the contemporary
poet find uncorrupted words to express the dreadful insights
his experience has given him? In the poem "In the Middle of
Life" Różewicz describes the poet-survivor's task as the recon-
struction anew, as it were, of the entire world around him. Absolutely nothing can be taken for granted: objects and ideas
must be named and learned once more:[13]

> After the end of the world
> after death
> I found myself in the middle of life
> I was creating myself
> I was building life
> people animals landscapes
>
> this is a table I said
> this is a table
> on the table are bread a knife
> a knife is used to cut bread
> people are nourished by bread
>
> one must love man
> I learned by day and night
> what must one love
> I answered man

Po końcu świata / po śmierci / znalazłem się w środku życia / stwarz-
ałem siebie / budowałem życie / ludzi zwierzęta krajobrazy / / to jest
stół mówiłem / to jest stół / na stole leży chleb nóż / nóż służy do kraj-
ania chleba / chlebem karmią się ludzie / / człowieka trzeba kochać /
uczyłem się w nocy w dzień / co trzeba kochać / odpowiadałem
człowieka.

IV A Struggle for Breath

Having returned from his optimistic detour to his fundamental
skepticism toward civilized existence in the postholocaust world,
during the past two decades Różewicz has dealt obsessively with
the question of the poet's disorientation in the modern world.
Unlike his predecessors, the contemporary poet, in Różewicz's
view, cannot sing blithely of the world around him; absolutely

everything he sees is tainted by his intimate knowledge of the degradation of the human soul. If the poets of old could sing of the beauty of a tree, for example (one thinks of Kochanowski's splendid poems to his linden tree), the poet of today thinks of a tree and sees a tortured body hanging in its branches.[14] The tried-and-true poetic forms which served generations of poets now attack the creator who would try to use them, crushing him so fiercely that even his silence cannot be heard through them.[15] Różewicz offers this definition: "Contemporary poetry / is a struggle for breath" ("Poezja współczesna / to walka o oddech").[16]

Różewicz is haunted by the belief that poetry is useless, that it is unwanted, dying out. And yet, despite his conviction that as a poet he is a living dead man and that creating poetry is akin to committing suicide, he finds himself driven to speak.[17] Silence has never been Różewicz's solution. In "A Pathetic Joke" he asserts himself defiantly:[18]

> I shall speak to all those people
> who don't read me
> don't hear don't know
> don't need me

only to conclude on a characteristically self-mocking note: "They don't need me / but I need them" ("będę mówił do wszystkich / którzy mnie nie czytają / nie słuchają nie znają / nie potrzebują / Oni mnie nie potrzebują / ale ja ich potrzebuję").

Różewicz's most famous description of the pitiable inadequacy of the modern poet appears in his gripping "Conversation with the Prince," in which the poet assumes the role of a garrulous Polonius:[19]

> Prince
> I am not a clerk
> I am a contemporary
> poet
> it is 1958
> you are curious what does
> a contemporary poet do

> Indifferent he speaks
> to the indifferent
> blinded he signs
> to the sightless
> he laughs and
> barks in his sleep
> awakened
> he cries
> he is made of rungs
> but he is not Jacob's ladder
> he is a voice without an echo
> a burden without weight
> a jester without a king

Książę / nie jestem urzędnikiem / jestem poetą / współczesnym / mamy rok 1958 / jesteś ciekawy / co robi / poeta współczesny / / Obojętny mówi do obojętnych / oślepiony daje znaki / niewidomym / śmieje się i / szczeka przez sen / obudzony / płacze / składa się ze szczebli / ale nie jest drabiną Jakubową / jest głosem bez echa / ciężarem bez wagi / błaznem bez króla

In an essay on contemporary poetry written at about the same time as "Conversation with the Prince" Różewicz restates this position. The poet, he declares, is more sensitive than most people to man's weakness in the modern world. Pressured by the public to adopt the roles of entertainer and freak-show attraction, his despairing response is to babble the nonsense which is poetry.[20] Behind such despair, of course, lies an unacknowledged arrogant belief in the poet's superiority to the masses, which makes a strange accompaniment to Różewicz's repeated insistence on the poet's closeness to mass man.

V *Antipoetry*

Although Różewicz's anguish has not led to its logical outcome —silence, one of its results has been his experimentation with new forms of poetry. Chief among these has been his rejection of the decorative devices of more traditional poetic practice. The typical Różewicz poem is a blunt, forthright statement which may derive its impact from the rawness of the writer's emotion (as in "Leave

Us Alone"), from the dramatic juxtaposition of opposites (as in the numerous poems which contrast the drive toward oblivion experienced by the living with the recent sufferings of the dead) or from the caricatured portrayal of the targets of his righteous hostility.

Różewicz is particularly fond of this latter means of directing his reader's response. For example, his moralistic animus against the self-satisfied petty bourgeois is demonstrated in the early poem "The Bill" in which he contemptuously depicts elegant ladies stuffing themselves on pastries in a fashionable café shortly after war's end.[21] It is also present in the later "Little Lyrical Announcements" in which self-centered intellectuals are shown sitting around in cafés groaning over their own fates in an exhibitionistic contemplation of their navels.[22] In contrast to these harsh caricatures, Różewicz can be equally insistent on manipulating his readers' emotions to acknowledge goodness where he sees it. In poems with such intent he ranges from the cloying sentimentality of "Quicker than in a Dream," in which the building of good housing for miners' children under socialism is described, to the more subtle coaxing toward acceptance of his viewpoint in "Dithyramb in Honor of Mothers-in-Law."[23] In "Dithyramb" Różewicz takes issue with the tradition of mother-in-law jokes and enumerates all the good and helpful prosaic tasks these wonderful old women perform in order to ease their children's and grandchildren's lives. "Dithyramb" is a variation on his theme of old women as patient, self-sacrificing, suffering witnesses to the world's endless cruelties.

Blunt statement and manipulation of the reader's emotional response are prime devices of Różewicz's "antipoetry." Lack of punctuation and exceedingly short lines make the printed poems appear radically different from "real" poetry, but Różewicz does employ a number of traditional devices of poetic organization, too. He rarely uses rhyme, metrical schemes, and pretty imagery, but his poems are by no means prose statements with only a typographical resemblance to poetry. Chief among his poetic devices is repetition, which he uses both for emphasis and coherence. Often entire lines or individual phrases are repeated. In some poems, the ending will repeat the opening lines (e.g., in "The Survivor" and "Leave Us Alone"), forcing the reader to re-

evaluate the beginning of the poem on the basis of what has
intervened.

Another traditional device which Różewicz employs quite
frequently is parallelism, which he may use to compare or contrast two subjects. This may be quite crude, as in the early poem
"Rose" which is based on the contrast between a vibrant flower
and a woman named Rose who was killed during the war.[24] A
frequent topic for contrast is the difference between traditional
and modern poets (e.g., "The Tree").[25] In Różewicz's later, more
intellectual poems, the device of contrast becomes less a matter
of structure and more a matter of philosophical implications—
a contrasting of "what is" with an unspecified "what might have
been" or "what ought to be." All of these devices and poetic
strategies are well suited to Różewicz's moralistic aims. He may
despair at the ultimate meaning of poetry, but nonetheless he
believes firmly that the poet's justification and duty reside in his
speaking the truth to modern man.

VI *The Voice of Anonymous Man*

Since about 1960 Różewicz has also occasionally experimented
with what he calls "the voice of anonymous man." If, early in his
career, he strove to be the voice of his generation, in these later
poems he seeks to efface himself as poet entirely. Rather than
present himself as a spokesman for a particular personal or gen-
erational point of view, he assumes the role of a recording device.
Poems written in this "anonymous voice" include "From the Diary
of a Soldier," which is presented as fragments of a Russian medic's
World War I diary and "White Polka Dots," which is a transcribed
missing persons report concerning the disappearance of an old
lady.[26]

A less extreme (and more fruitful) use of this anonymous
reportorial device is the construction of poems out of factual
fragments, a montagelike approach to the building of poetry by
reference to events, cultural phenomena, newspaper ads, and so
forth, which date from and give the flavor of a particular era.
"The World 1906" and "Fragments from the Interwar Years" are
representative of this direction in Różewicz's experimentation.[27]
Such poetry is not an innovation, of course; the inclusion of docu-

mentary material in artistic works is a basic device of modern art. Różewicz, however, can be credited with renewing its popularity in post-1956 Polish poetry. Though he soon went beyond it, the device can be found as a characteristic component in the works of other contemporary poets, most notably that of Miron Białoszewski.

VII *Spokesman for the Self*

Różewicz's experimentation with anonymous voices turned out, in the final analysis, to be a dead end for him. His last two collections of poetry, *Twarz trzecia* (Face III, 1968) and *Regio* (1969), are intensely personal statements. Many of the poems in these volumes deal frankly with such traditional concerns of lyrical poets as the fear of death, erotic fantasies, memories of past loves, and the loss of loved ones. In "Among So Many Concerns" Różewicz adopts a characteristically jaunty attitude to express his preoccupation with dying and the superficiality of our daily concerns:[28]

> Among many concerns
> very urgent
> I forgot about the fact
> that one must also
> be dying
>
> scatterbrained
> I've neglected this duty
> or fulfilled it
> superficially
>
> starting tomorrow
> everything will change
>
> I shall begin to die carefully
> wisely optimistically
> without wasting time

Wśród wielu zajęć / bardzo pilnych / zapomniałem o tym / że również trzeba / umierać / / lekkomyślny / zaniedbałem ten obowiązek /

lub wypełniałem go / powierzchownie / / od jutra / wszystko się zmieni / / zacznę umierać starannie / mądrze optymistycznie / bez straty czasu.

Różewicz's major poetic works from the 1960s are his long poems, "Et in arcadia ego," "Falling," and "Non-Stop-Shows."[29] In all three works, Różewicz merges his private and his public concerns. All represent a confrontation of Różewicz, the war-scarred private citizen of an Eastern European country, with Western European postwar culture. In "Et in arcadia ego" ("And I too was in Arcady") Różewicz depicts himself as a wide-eyed northern traveler to Italy, seeking the golden land of harmony, sunshine, and innocent happiness that literary tradition, going back to Goethe, has located in this southern country. What he finds, instead, on his journey through Naples, Florence, Rome, and Venice is a land of great beauty which is lacking in moral sensitivity—a tourist haven in which people escape from the lessons which the Hitler years should have made obvious. Written as a traveler's diary, the poem is full of sensual detail about the sights and smells of the Italian scene, interspersed with private musings on the nature of twentieth-century existence. It ends on a quiet, sad note which emphasizes the futility of seeking for spiritual peace:[30]

> I'm not ashamed
> I cried in that country
>
> the beauty moved me
>
> I was a child once more
> in the bosom of the land
> I cried
> I'm not ashamed
>
> I tried to return to paradise

Nie wstydzę się / płakałem w tym kraju / / piękno dotknęło mnie / / byłem znów dzieckiem / w łonie tego kraju / płakałem / nie wstydzę się / / Próbowałem wrócić do raju.

Neither "Falling" nor "Non-Stop-Shows" shares with "Et in arcadia ego" its somber regret for the shattered dream of a golden age. These two poems are savage indictments of contemporary Western civilization, couched in a breathless torrent of hostility. In "Falling" Różewicz insists on the moral degeneracy of contemporary man by a series of allusions to such "outmoded" moralists as St. Augustine, Dostoevsky, and Camus who could still, in their charming innocence, entertain the notion of sin. Modern man, he argues, has seen so much of vice that there are no more moral guidelines; one no longer has even a sense of what it is to be damned:[31]

> the word falling is not
> the right word
> it does not explain that movement
> of body and soul
> with which the man of today
> passeth away
>
> rebels
> angels damned
> used to fall headfirst
> the man of today
> falls in all directions
> simultaneously
> . . . . .
>
> at one time people fell
> and rose
> vertically
> nowadays
> people fall
> horizontally

słowo spadanie nie jest / słowem właściwym / nie objaśnia tego ruchu / ciała i duszy / w którym przemija / człowiek współczesny / / zbuntowani ludzie / potępione anioły / spadały głową w dół / człowiek współczesny / spada we wszystkich kierunkach / równocześnie / . . . / / dawniej spadano / i wznoszono się / pionowo / obecnie / spada się / poziomo.

"Non-Stop-Shows" is written with the same intense rage against the tempo of our frenzied civilization which allows man to abnegate his moral responsibilities to the future. Unlike "Falling" this poem is also a clear expression of personal frustration:[32]

> To write in our times
> you have to delimit compromise isolate
> deafen yourself
> people used to write from an excess
> today from a lack
> The possibilities of the man of today are immense
> they depend on constant anxiety
> whether it's not too late
> for love for the study of esperanto for travel
> for writing a novel for children for beauty
> for faith for love for death
> We are immensely busy
> We do not know our own children.

Żeby pisać w naszych czasach / trzeba się ograniczyć zgodzić zamknąć / ogłuszyć / dawniej pisano z nadmiaru / dziś z braku / Możliwości współczesnego człowieka są ogromne / polegają one na ciągłym niepokoju / czy nie za późno / na miłość na naukę esperanto na podróże / na pisanie powieści na dzieci na piękno / na wiarę na życie na śmierć / Jesteśmy ogromnie zajęci / Nie znamy własnych dzieci. . . .

In its frenzied haste to escape from the fear of time running out, of inevitable death, contemporary civilization has come up with the anodyne of the movies. In a virtuoso performance which mimics the cinematic speed of the modern life which he rejects, Różewicz creates a whirling panorama of contemporary preoccupations with sex, pornography, entertainment, and self-indulgence in every form. To project this vision he uses his old device of enumerating objects, but now they are no longer the simple staples of life (bread, knife, table) but the names which flash across Europe in neon lights:[33]

> Munich München
> Italia Bar Harem-Bar Haremsfrauen
> Bongo Bar Tai-Tung Beste Koche aus Chungking
> La Bohème Shashlik Bockwurst Riesenwurst

Intermezzo Striptease à la Paris
Moulin Rouge Bomben Variétéprogramm
Die Zwiebel Lola Montez Bar Pique Dame. . . .

It comes as something of a surprise that at the end of this contemptuous diatribe against modern culture, Różewicz arrives at the decision that one cannot turn one's back on one's age. The luxury of retreating to spiritual seclusion is also a thing of the past. As a modern poet, the writer must reconcile himself (since poetry persists despite his earlier predictions of its imminent demise) and maintain his ties with life. In a burst of mock enthusiasm, Różewicz ends his poem by promising to take up this new burden:[34]

now I am to return and press my face
close my eyes and lips stop up my ears with wax
an optimistic nice
pure poet.

teraz mam wrócić i przycisnąć moją twarz / zamknąć oczy i usta zalepić uszy woskiem / optymistyczny miły / czysty poeta.

VIII *Conclusion*

As the sarcasm of the closing lines of "Non-Stop-Shows" indicates, Różewicz cannot turn himself into a "nice poet" simply by an effort of will. Neither can he shake off the anxiety and despair which (except for the brief interlude of Communist optimism) have always marked his poetry, whether it was assigned to his generation, to an anonymous voice from the masses, or was frankly acknowledged as his private woe. Różewicz continues to express his belief that modern man is trapped in a crazy world amid people who refuse to acknowledge the tragedy of life.

During the last ten to fifteen years, Różewicz's most forceful expression of this outlook has been consigned to plays and short stories. He has become a provocative practitioner of the theater of the absurd. His plays and theoretical pronouncements test the limits imposed by theatrical tradition and staging techniques. Perhaps by virtue of its stubborn clinging to life, poetry, whose death he has so long prophesied, has become a dead end for him. This is evidenced, most poignantly, by the fact that much of his later poetry appears to be a reworking and imitation of the younger Różewicz.

CHAPTER 6

Wisława Szymborska:
The Masking of Despair

WISŁAWA SZYMBORSKA is also a member of the generation
of writers who were born during the early 1920s. Like
Różewicz, she, too, has derived from her experience of World
War II and a later disillusionment with Stalinist politics a cynical
mistrust of the supposedly civilizing aspects of Western culture.
Szymborska shares her generation's contemptuous dismissal of
any exaggerated claims for poetry's humane powers. Like Białoszewski and Różewicz, she is suspicious of inflated language,
false sentiment, and pretty imagery. Her cynicism, however, is
tempered by a belief in rational discourse, and the result is a
poetic style which is distinctly different from that of her fellow
poets. There is no fragmentation of language in Szymborska's
poetry; rather, using colloquial language and, frequently, the
most conventional of settings, her poems present coherent drama-
tizations of compelling philosophical issues.

I Biographical Note and Early Work

Szymborska was born in 1923 in the small town of Bnin in
western Poland. However, as a poet and literary critic she is
associated with the city of Cracow where she completed her
university studies (in Polish philology and sociology) and where
she has lived and worked for all of her adult life. She has been
associated, in various capacities, with the literary newspaper
Życie Literackie (Literary Life) since 1952, when she joined
the editorial staff of its poetry section.

Szymborska made her literary debut immediately after the

war with a poem published in the Cracow newspaper, *Dziennik Polski* (Polish Daily). From 1945 through 1948 she published approximately thirty poems in this newspaper. Their main theme was, as might be expected, the war and the German occupation. In these poems Szymborska expressed her feelings of guilt at being a survivor and her deep mourning for the violated land. A collection of these early poems was slated for publication in 1949, but the plans were canceled when Szymborska became the butt of political attacks by Communist literary hatchetmen. Under the newly imposed strictures of socialist realism in the arts, Szymborska was accused of writing poetry which was inaccessible to the common people and so morbidly obsessed with the war as to be unsuitable for publication in the forward-looking Polish People's Republic. Some of these early poems have been included by Szymborska in post-1956 editions of her poetry; others remain unpublished.[1]

Some Polish poets (Białoszewski and Herbert, for example) responded to the Stalinist demands on literature by what has come to be called "internal emigration"—silence, or "writing for the drawer". Szymborska, however, like Różewicz, rethought her position and began to write poems which were politically correct and blatantly propagandistic. These poems were published in two volumes, *Dlatego żyjemy* (That's Why We Live, 1952; second edition, 1954) and *Pytania zadawane sobie* (Questions to Oneself, 1954). The poems in these collections tend to strident expressions of almost hysterical hatred for the old order, imperialist warmongers, and other contemporary targets of Stalinist propaganda, and are vastly inferior to Szymborska's post-1956 poetry. "Old Working Woman," for example, is a melodramatic recitation in which an elderly woman speaks of her sufferings under the capitalist system. She had been fired from her miserable job because of her pregnancy, had attempted suicide, survived, but lost the baby.[2] The piling on of tragedy in this work is reminiscent of the pathetic excesses of mid-nineteenth century naturalistic literature. A more militant note is sounded in other poems, such as "Song about a War Criminal," which is an enraged protest against the release of Nazi war criminals from Allied prisons.[3] "From Korea" fits into the

anti-American campaign of the Korean War with what purports
to be an eyewitness account of an American soldier putting out
the eyes of a Korean civilian.[4]

That Szymborska has since disavowed these works, along with
her dogmatic politics of the Stalinist period, is clear, since she
included only nine poems from *That's Why We Live* and *Questions to Oneself* in her retrospective volume, *Wiersze wybrane*
(Selected Poems, 1964) and none at all in the 1970 collection,
Poezje (Poetry). In "Rehabilitation," a poem published in her
first post-Thaw volume, Szymborska confessed she had been
guilty of believing that people condemned by the Communist
hierarchy were really traitors and asserted that her helplessness
before these victims now heightened her consciousness of the
ultimate futility of poetry which can make no reparations to the
dead.[5]

II   Calling to the Yeti: *A Transitional Work*

In the more than two decades since the Polish Thaw, Szymborska has published five slender volumes of poetry and two
editions of selected poems.[6] The first of her post-Thaw books,
Wołanie do Yeti (Calling to the Yeti, 1957), is clearly a transitional work. In it Szymborska returned to the war themes that
had haunted her in the late 1940s (in "Still," for example);
apologized, in effect, for her own poetic and political excesses
(in the above-mentioned "Rehabilitation"); looked back to her
childhood to weigh the effects of her Catholic upbringing (in
such poems as "Night" and "A Meeting"); and, most important,
exhibited in a few works the tersely ironic style for which her
poetry is valued today.

Two poems from this collection are particularly noteworthy
as early instances of Szymborska's preoccupation with the question of the value of civilization. In "From An Expedition to the
Himalayas Which Did Not Take Place" Szymborska addresses
the Yeti (the legendary Abominable Snowman), explaining to
this creature of the frozen heights what characterizes the life
of man below. She offers a catalog of ordinary things which
make up contemporary civilization—items such as bread, the
alphabet, and basic arithmetic. Szymborska continues her enu-

meration of man's "accomplishments" with an ironic, and not particularly subtle, juxtaposition of high cultural achievements with individual crimes and the violent course of history:[7]

> Yeti, not only crimes
> are possible among us.
> Yeti, not all words
> are death sentences.
>
> We inherit hope—
> the gift of forgetfulness.
> You notice how we give birth
> to children among the ruins.
>
> Yeti, we have Shakespeares.
> Yeti, we play violins.
> Yeti, when darkness falls
> we turn on lights.

Yeti, nie tylko zbrodnie / są u nas możliwe. / Yeti, nie wszystkie słowa / skazują na śmierć. / / Dziedziczymy nadzieję– / dar zapominania. / Zobaczysz, jak rodzimy / dzieci na ruinach. / / Yeti, Szekspiry mamy. / Yeti, na skrzypcach gramy. / Yeti, o zmroku / zapalamy światło.

Although the argument of "From an Expedition" points forward to Szymborska's many poems on civilization, the style is closer to the overinsistence and heavy-handedness of her earlier work.

A similar theme is explored in another poem from *Calling to the Yeti*—"Two Monkeys by Bruegel"—but in it Szymborska employs what has by now become her characteristic device of encapsulating a philosophical proposition in a wittily narrated anecdote:[8]

> Here's what my great dream of my final exam is like:
> two chained monkeys are sitting in a window,
> the sky is fluttering outside
> and the ocean is bathing.
>
> I'm being examined on human history.
> I stammer and cast about for words.

One monkey, staring at me, listens ironically;
the other appears to be dozing—
but when silence descends after a question
he coaches me
with the soft rattling of his chain.

Tak wygląda mój wielki maturalny sen: / siedzą w oknie dwie małpy przykute łańcuchem, / za oknem fruwa niebo / i kąpie się morze. / / Zdaję z historii ludzi. / Jąkam się i brnę. / / Małpa, wpatrzona we mnie, ironicznie słucha, / druga niby to drzemie— / a kiedy po pytaniu nastaje milczenie, / podpowiada mi / cichym brząkaniem łańcucha.

Since "Two Monkeys by Bruegel" exemplifies the poetic style which marks Szymborska's mature works, let us look at it more closely. It is, on the surface, simply a neatly told anecdote reflecting a familiar situation. Who, after all, has not at some time dreamed of failing an important test? The two monkeys who supply the philosophical point of the poem slip in almost unnoticed. The reader can be expected to accept a slight distortion of realia if the event is specifically labeled a dream.

The monkeys, however, are not figments of the speaker's imagination, although they have been incorporated into her fantasy world. They are, as the title of the poem suggests, the unusual subjects of a Pieter Bruegel canvas (dated 1562). In the painting two monkeys are attached by a chain to a ring set in a windowsill overlooking Antwerp harbor. Sky and water are visible through the window, as are the faint outlines of ships at anchor, a flock of birds in flight, some windmills and other buildings whose flimsiness contrasts with the sturdy stonework of the building which is, for the monkeys, a prison. There are no people in this landscape beyond the window. One monkey is looking out on this scene; the other looks into the room in which the viewer presumably stands. Both monkeys are directing their glances downward, not, as Szymborska implies, toward the observer. The "correct" interpretation of Bruegel's painting is something of a puzzle, and Szymborska is here offering her own response to its deeper meaning and at the same time incorporating it as supporting evidence into her own view of human history.

The anecdote is presented in an offhand manner by an "I" (of indeterminate gender here, although Szymborska's lyric persona is usually female) who addresses the reader in collo- quial sentences echoing the rhythms of the spoken language. The lines of verse are of uneven length, seemingly regulated by syntactic constraints alone, and with only the faintest hints of rhyme. A metrical scheme is present, however, which dis- creetly regulates the flow of the lines.[9] Szymborska's discretion in adapting traditional prosodic rules is matched by the tact with which she gives voice here to one of her most firmly held convictions: that the history of mankind is endlessly dismal. Her achievement in "Two Monkeys" is even more impressive when it is contrasted with the rhetorical blatancy of the con- temporary "From an Expedition."

Szymborska is not a writer whose every collection brings to light new thematic or stylistic preoccupations. The best of her poems since 1957 have demonstrated, instead, a refinement of the careful use of irony and the poetic restraint already observed in "Two Monkeys." The majority of the poems in the books she has published since *Calling to the Yeti—Sól* (Salt, 1962), *Sto pociech* (A Barrel of Laughs, 1967), *Wszelki wypadek* (Any Event, 1972), and *Wielka liczba* (Large Number, 1976)—explore a limited number of themes, all corollaries of her existentialist conviction that each man stands alone in an uncaring, capricious universe. These volumes include lyric poems which focus deli- cately on the impassable distance between the closest of lovers; disquisitions on civilization and evolution by an observer who is cognizant of the broad sweep of natural and human history into which the present is absorbed; and ironic commentaries on the inadequacies of poetry and its limited contemporary appeal.

III *The Pain of Love*

In a typical love poem by Szymborska, the woman speaker is trying to come to terms either with the painful emotions she has experienced at an actual parting from her loved one or with the realization that she can never bridge the psychological dis- tance which separates them. Often the feminine speaker avoids

98 CONTEMPORARY POLISH POETRY

direct expression of too raw emotions by the evasive tactics of
irony or buffoonery.

The poem "Shadow" begins with the simple declaration: "My
shadow is like a jester behind a queen," and from there the
metaphor of a royal triangle of king, queen, knave (in which
the latter is the queen's own shadow) takes over and expands
into a conceit. The jester, who is a shadow, must mimic every
one of the queen's motions, but in his two-dimensional existence
her most innocent movements are distorted into suicidal gestures.
When the queen gets out of a chair, the jester/shadow on the
wall inevitably strikes his head against the ceiling. If the queen
looks out of her window, the jester leaps to the ground. The
queen is alert to the dangers confronting her jester. She promises
that she will be especially solicitous of his safety when she bids
farewell to her beloved king at a railroad station. She knows,
however, that despite her precautions the jester will dramatize
her pain by turning her gestures into a suicidal motion:[10]

> I shall be ever so light when I move my arms,
> ever so light when I turn my head,
> at our parting, king,
> at the station, king.
>
> It's the jester, king,
> will lie down on the tracks at that moment.

Będę, ach, lekka w ruchu ramion, / ach, lekka w odwróceniu głowy, /
królu, przy naszym pożegnaniu, / królu, na stacji kolejowej. / / Królu,
to błazen o tej porze, / królu, położe się na torze.

Szymborska's efforts at disguising the woman's sentiments in
"Shadow" in a kind of poetic masquerade run the grave risk of
appearing rather too precious. This is a serious problem in a
number of her poems. She is more successful in her love poetry
when she adopts a completely mocking stance, as in "Buffo," or
when she permits her heroine to speak directly, without any
evasive donning of masks (as in "I am too close" or "Over wine").
In "Buffo" the speaker looks at herself and her lover from the
perspective of a century or more in the future and imagines how

actors in time to come could stage a successful farce based on their relationship.[11] In "I am too close" a woman, lying in bed with her sleeping husband or lover, muses on how their intimacy is itself the wedge between them:[12]

> I am too close to appear in his dreams.
> I do not flutter over him, nor evade him
> beneath the roots of trees. I am too close.
>
> . . . .
>
> . . . He is sleeping,
> more accessible at this moment to the cashier of
>   a wandering one-lion circus
> whom he saw once in his life
> than to me who am lying beside him.

Jestem za blisko, żeby mu się śnić. / Nie fruwam nad nim, nie uciekam mu / pod korzeniami drzew. Jestem za blisko. / . . . / . . . On śpi, / w tej chwili dostępniejszy widzianej raz w życiu / kasjerce wędrowego cyrku z jednym lwem / niż mnie leżącej obok.

What is bright and animated in this poem derives from the woman's vivid imagination of the man's possible fantasies, while her pain finds its expression only in the austere, insistently repeated phrase, "I am too close."

"Over wine" explores from a somewhat different perspective the same theme of love which founders on reality and lack of mystery. The woman of this poem is aware of herself as a void, a nullity given identity only by the imagination and needs of her lover:[13]

> A table is a table, wine is wine
> in a goblet, which is a goblet
> and stands there standing on the table.
> But I am imaginary,
> unbelievably imaginary,
> imaginary even to my very blood.
>
> . . . .
>
> When he isn't looking at me
> I seek my reflection
> on the wall. And see only
> a nail, from which the picture has been removed.

Stół jest stołem, wino winem / w kieliszku, co jest kieliszkiem / i stoi
stojąc na stole. / A ja jestem urojona, / urojona nie do wiary, / urojona aż do krwi. / / . . . / / Kiedy on nie patrzy na mnie, / szukam
swego odbicia / na ścianie. I widzę tylko / gwóźdź, z którego zdjęto
obraz.

The theme of "Over wine" is the same haunting message which
underlies all of Szymborska's poems on abandoned and lonely
women: a woman is an empty vessel dependent for her very
identity on the life-giving force of a man's love. Like many women
poets, Szymborska writes only of the love between man and
woman; never do we find in her work the supposedly feminine
theme of motherhood. When a nurturing, "maternal" note does
appear in her poetry, it is only in relation to an adult male who
arouses her tenderness and pity.

Since 1970 a new attitude toward love has appeared in Szymborska's poetry. The surprising gentleness of "Homecomings," in
which an exhausted, harried scientist is tenderly watched over
by his wife as he curls up under his blankets like a huge, formally
dressed fetus, is symptomatic of this change.[14] It can be seen, too,
in "Happy Love," in which Szymborska turns her characteristic
sarcasm to a defense of love and an attack on the prosaic majority
who think true love is an impossible ideal.[15] This softened attitude, a romanticism still clothed in irony, corresponds to the
generally more tolerant tone of *Any Event* and *Large Number*.
Indeed, in *Large Number* the themes of abandonment and the
pain of love are conspicuously absent.

IV   *The Meaning of Existence*

A major theme of Szymborska's poetry, which links her mature
work with the concerns, although not the posture, of her Stalinist
poems, is her persistent interest in the evolutionary and historical
processes whose result is contemporary civilization. Her general
attitude, as indicated in "Two of Breugel's Monkeys," is pes-
simistic. The history of mankind, despite some luminous cultural
achievements, is a dreary one. Moreover, despite the object
lessons it might offer, history is, as a rule, ignored.

In "From an Expedition to the Himalayas Which Did Not Take

Place" Szymborska had spoken of humanity's refusal to learn
from or be defeated by the past: "we give birth to children
among the ruins." This theme is pursued and refined in the
haunting "Monologue for Cassandra." Cassandra delivers her
monologue long after the fall of Troy as she looks at the ruins of
her city and remembers with what terror and loathing her people
listened to her prophecies. There is no pleasure for Cassandra in
history's verification of her prophetic vision. Rather, as she recol-
lects the hope to which her people stubbornly clung, Cassandra
regrets her clear-sightedness and rejects that ability to envision
the course of history which separated her from the ordinary life
of her people. Since it is ineffectual anyway, the gift of prophesy
is a curse:[16]

> I loved them.
> But I loved them from on high.
> From above life.
> From the future. Where it is always empty
> and where there is nothing so easy as seeing death.
> I regret that my voice was hard.
> Look at yourselves from the stars, I cried,
> look at yourselves from the stars.
> They heard me and lowered their eyes.
>
> .   .   .   .
>
> It turned out as I said.
> But that proves nothing.
> This is my flame-charred robe.
> These are my prophetic rags.
> And this is my contorted face.
> A face which did not know that it could be beautiful.

Kochałam ich. / Ale kochałam z wysoka. / Sponad życia. / Z przysz-
łości. / Gdzie zawsze jest pusto / i skąd cóż łatwiejszego jak zobaczyć
śmierć. / Żałuję że mój głos był twardy. / Spójrzcie na siebie z gwiazd
—wołałam— / spójrzcie na siebie z gwiazd. / Słyszeli i spuszczali oczy. /
/ . . . / / Wyszło na moje. / Tylko że z tego nie wynika nic. / A to jest
moja szatka ogniem osmalona. / A to są moje prorockie rupiecie. / A to
jest moja wykrzywiona twarz. / Twarz, która nie wiedziała, że mogła
być piękna.

Szymborska uses many of the same devices which she employs

in her love lyrics in her poems on the accidental nature of human existence. In addition to the direct emotional statement of such works as "Monologue for Cassandra" she also makes use of irony, with its concomitant distancing of the observer from her subject. Although her philosophical poems do not share either the depth or the discursiveness of Zbigniew Herbert's work, she shares with him a predilection for employing the rhythms of an educated person's spoken language.

Both her use of self-directed irony and her colloquial style are demonstrated in "Wonder," a poem on the mystery of existence:[17]

> Why in an excessively single person?
> Why this one and not that? And what am I doing here?
> On a day which is Tuesday? In a house, not a nest?
> In a skin and not scales? With a face and not leaves?
>
> . . . .
> . . . Why
> neither next door nor a hundred miles from here,
> neither yesterday nor a hundred years ago,
> do I sit here staring into a dark corner
> like that growling creature called a dog,
> watching with suddenly lifted head?

Czemu w zanadto jednej osobie? / Tej a nie innej? I co tu robię? / W dzień co jest wtorkiem? / W domu nie gnieździe? / W skórze nie łusce? Z twarzą, nie liściem? / . . . / . . . Czemu / nie obok ani sto mil stąd, / nie wczoraj, ani sto lat temu / siedzę i patrzę w ciemny kąt / —tak jak z wzniesionym nagle łbem / patrzy warczące zwane psem?

A different use of ironic distancing is exemplified in the title poem of *Any Event*, in which Szymborska simply lists a long series of words which language provides as a substitute for true understanding. Her approach is designed to undermine the authority of language by relying on the effect created by a catalog of contradictory "explanations," all fraudulently masquerading as "the truth."[18]

The preciousness which sometimes mars Szymborska's love poetry also surfaces on occasion in her serious poems on human existence. Szymborska likes to tease, linking playfulness with irony as a way of controlling the emotional impact of her poignant thoughts. For example, in "Discovery" she begins by giving voice to a stubborn belief in human progress which she claims to hold despite the awesome might of science and its threat to the world's continued existence. With words of firm conviction which echo the avowal of faith in the Creed—"I believe in a great discovery. / I believe in the man who will make the discovery. / I believe in the terror of the man who will make the discovery"—Szymborska describes a future great event in the moral development of mankind. Some day a scientist will make a major discovery, but realizing that its potential for harm is overwhelming, this ambitious man will destroy all evidence pointing to his work, will sacrifice his career for the benefit of mankind, and will take his terrible secret to the grave. Having created this scenario by means of her reiterated "credo" (twelve of the twenty-nine lines of the poem begin with the words "I believe"), Szymborska goes on to undermine her feigned credulity with words of searing self mockery: "My faith is strong, blind, and unfounded" ("Moja wiara jest silna, ślepa i bez podstaw").[19]

V *Conclusion*

Szymborska's skepticism has not been so corrosive as to undermine completely her faith in either the communicative function of language or the persuasive power of poetry. Her frustration at the limitations of language and human understanding is, in part, a product of her highly developed awareness of the inexpressible richness of life. "Under a Single Star," which she has twice placed in the significant final position of a collection of poetry (in both *Poems* and *Any Event*), testifies to the joy Szymborska still derives from the fullness of existence despite her rationally determined pessimism. It is, as well, a sensible appreciation of her own poetic style:[20]

I apologize to everything that I cannot be everywhere.
I apologize to everyone that I cannot be every man and woman.
I know that so long as I live nothing can justify me
because I am an obstacle to myself.

Don't be angry with me, language, because I use pathetic words
and labor at making them seem light.

Przepraszam wszystko, że nie mogę być wszędzie. / Przepraszam
wszystkich, że nie umiem być każdym i każdą. / Wiem, że póki żyję,
nic mnie nie usprawiedliwia, / ponieważ sama sobie stoję na przeszkod-
zie. / Nie miej mi za złe, mowo, że pożyczam patetycznych słów, / a
potem trudu dokładam, żeby wydały się lekkie.

Since abandoning the rhetoric of propaganda of her first two
volumes of poetry, Szymborska has become a quieter, philosophical poet. She explores, usually from a woman's perspective, the
poignancy of human isolation while celebrating, as a poet, the
life-affirming drive to creativity. Her style, at its best, is concise
and understated, though a tendency to exaggerated irony and
a rhetoric of negation is a frequent threat to its perfection. Szymborska prefers to set philosophical issues in a frame of scenes
from everyday life, describing them in unstrained, colloquial
language. Her often ironic stance, based on a wry, mocking
humor, effectively counterbalances the somber implications of
her message.

CHAPTER 7

Miron Białoszewski: Poet of the Prosaic

MANY superficial similarities link Miron Białoszewski with Tadeusz Różewicz. Like Różewicz, Białoszewski belongs to the generation of the 1920s. He, too, has made a radical break with the traditions of Polish poetry. Białoszewski's antipoetry, however, has developed in a different direction from Różewicz's, and although the latter poet has had many imitators in Poland, Białoszewski is not one of them. His work in theater, poetry, and prose has clearly followed a unique path of development.

I Biographical Note

Białoszewski was born in Warsaw in 1922 and has lived there for most of his life. His writing is closely identified with Poland's capital. The city's streets and monuments, the author's own apartment, daily events in the lives of ordinary citizens, and the rhythms of Warsaw speech are the building blocks of Białoszewski's poetry and prose. His most successful work, the prose *Pamiętnik z powstania warszawskiego* (A Memoir of the Warsaw Uprising) is a devotional offering to his suffering native city.[1]

Białoszewski was raised in a working-class family. His father worked with the postal administration and his mother was a seamstress. His social origins may account in part for his interest in people on the margins of Polish urban society. He lived through the German occupation in the capital and experienced the Warsaw Uprising as a trapped civilian. One significant characteristic of his creative work—his antiheroic pragmatism, which abjures the grand gesture—was already adumbrated during the war years in his reluctance to engage in organized conspiratorial activity.

It is clear from Białoszewski's memoir that he was already writing (plays and stories) during the occupation, but some of these works were lost and none were published. After the war he worked as a journalist. He made his debut as a serious poet during the hospitable first year of the Thaw, when his volume of poetry, *Obroty rzeczy* (Revolutions of Things), appeared.[2] The Thaw period also marked his emergence as an experimental playwright, director, and actor. His tiny private theater, the Teatr Osobny, housed in a two-room apartment, was well-known in Warsaw intellectual circles. In 1959 the American journalist, Joseph Alsop, visited the Teatr Osobny and described it as follows:

> Nothing quite like this apartment exists
> anywhere else in the world. Every single
> piece of furniture has been gravely maimed or
> wounded at some time in the past. Abstract
> paintings, strange and menacing constructions
> of wire and masking tape, great numbers of
> fragments of Polish baroque church-sculpture,
> two damaged but still magical Polish-Byzantine
> icons, the remnants of a beautifully tender late
> Gothic altar piece—all these and many other
> objects are hung or strewn about.[3]

As we shall see, this museum of crippled objects is virtually the incarnation of Białoszewski's poetry.

During the more than two decades which have elapsed since Białoszewski's debut as a poet, he has published three more volumes of poetry, two books of prose fragments, his memoir of the Warsaw Uprising, and his theater pieces.[4] With each publication he has acquired a more controversial fame. Although critical arguments swirl around him, he shuns the limelight and employs an array of idiosyncracies as a shield against the uncongenial world of the famous.

Starting with his earliest work, Białoszewski's choice of themes has been outside the boundaries of traditional poetic subject matter. His approach to poetry has been irreverent and iconoclastic. Each of his four poetry collections is a renewed attack on, and attempted escape from, the strictures of poetic tradition. The last of these volumes, *Było i było* (It Was and It Was, 1965), includes a significant number of prose pieces. Since the publication of *It Was and It Was*, Białoszewski (again like Różewicz) has virtually abandoned poetry in favor of prose. Thus while still a productive writer, his published poetic works span only one decade, but the prose writings continue to shed light retrospectively on his poetry.

II *Things in Themselves*

The title of Białoszewski's first verse collection heralded the direction his poetry was to take. *Revolutions of Things* already reveals (although in less prosaic form than his later work) the fascination with objects, especially simple, homely items of daily use, which is one of the hallmarks of Białoszewski's art.

It is instructive to compare Białoszewski's treatment of ordinary objects with that of Różewicz. Różewicz has written, for instance, about a knife and a loaf of bread (in "In the Middle of Life"). In emphasizing the renewed peacetime function of a knife—to cut bread rather than serve as a murder weapon (the implied alternative)—Różewicz uses the knife as a carrier of an emotionally potent message which the speaker of his poem cannot bring himself to express directly. The laconic reference to the knife's function is a shorthand reminder of the speaker's distorted experiences before the return of peacetime and the creation of the poem. The knife and bread are therefore important to Różewicz as symbols of a human predicament.[5]

The slotted ladle in Białoszewski's "Gray Eminences of Rapture" carries no such burden. The poet is interested in the ladle as an object whose poetic dimensions have been overlooked in favor of its functional attributes:[6]

> How I rejoice
>   that you are both the heavens and a kaleidoscope,
>   that you have so many artificial stars,
>   that you shine so in the monstrance of luminosity,
>   when one lifts your hollowed-out
>   half-globe
>   in the air
>   near one's eyes.

How unstrained in wealth you are,
slotted ladle!

Jakże się cieszę, / że jesteś niebem i kalejdoskopem, / że masz tyle
sztucznych gwiazd, / że tak świecisz w monstrancji jasności, / gdy pod-
nieść twoje wydrążone / pół-globu / dokoła oczu, / pod powietrze. /
Jakżeś nieprzecedzona w bogactwie, / łyżko durszlakowa!

Białoszewski has written numerous poems on simple objects,
many of which, like "Gray Eminences of Rapture," seek to view
objects in a new light, divorced from their restrictive functional
roles. In "Self-Verified" he celebrates the multiplicity of form
which functional destruction may reveal:[7]

Here stands a chair:
an article of truth
the sculpture of itself
bound into a single sheaf
the abstraction of reality.

It is broken.
And this too is form
this way—a chandelier
that way—the face of a bull.

The abstract vocation of a chair
now attracts
whole crowds of reality
binds into a single sheaf
in the storehouse of truth
the reality of abstraction.

Stoi krzesło: / artykuł prawdy / rzeźba samego siebie / powiązana w
jeden pęk / abstrakcji rzeczywistości. / / Połamało się. / I to też forma
/ tak—świecznik / tak—mina byka. / / Abstrakcyjne powołanie krzesła
/ przyciąga teraz / całe tłumy rzeczywistości / wiąże w jeden pęk / w
składzie prawdy / rzeczywistość abstrakcji.

Białoszewski's exploitation of the poetic possibilities of household objects when they are released from the constraints of function is not limited to his poetry. It is basically a visual liberation,

a freeing of form from function, and as such it can be seen in his imaginative stage properties in the Teatr Osobny programs where, for example, a salt cellar becomes a chandelier in the miniature world of a finger-puppet show and an iron-mesh pot scrubber adorns a royal crown.[8] In the theater, it is true, Białoszewski had collaborators, and some of these clever inventions may not have originated with him.

Not all of Białoszewski's "thing poems" are devoted as purely to the object's reflection in a liberated imagination as these works are. In other poems, objects are intermeshed with human experience. Białoszewski may write about a noisy radiator, a banging shutter, or a leaking pipe. These things remain themselves in his poems and are not made to function as symbols of anything extrinsic. Some poems address objects with the emotional intensity usually reserved in lyric poetry for a beloved person; curiously, no conventional love lyrics exist among Białoszewski's poems. In still others the cool descriptions of objects conceal beneath their surface detachment a wealth of emotional associations. For example, in a cycle of poems devoted to his favorite quilt, Białoszewski offers us its genealogy:[9]

> for fourteen years
> I have slept thought eaten
> beneath one Carmel
> Carmel is a quilt
> this quilt was left by one Stefa
> her ghetto burned down[10]
> she lived here then she left it to me

czternaście lat / śpię myślę jem / pod jedną Karmel / Karmelą jest jedna kołdra / to kołdra jest po jednej Stefie / upiekło jej się getto / mieszkała to zostawiła mi.

Only with the publication of *A Memoir of the Warsaw Uprising* did it become clear that the "one Stefa" so casually introduced in this poem was a Jewish woman who hid with Białoszewski's family during the occupation and for whom he felt a deep affection.

Other poems reveal Białoszewski's underlying ambivalence

toward the objects which surround him. An abnormal, almost
paranoid, terror of the unpredictability of objects is revealed
in "Romance with the Concrete":[11]

> suddenly
> love
> for whom? for whom?
> with legs bent
> in the reverse of kneeling
> I confide
> in my chair
> first
> and there is emotion
> and mutual bending
> and now it is you
> oh chair
> I love you
> chair
> I love you
> and this is a tragic love
> because already there is
> the lurking of something other than the chair which has
>   been betrayed
> it will discover me
> it will espy me   it will be looking out
> it will take revenge

wtem / miłość / ku komu? ku komu? / nogami uginany / na odwrót
klęczek / krzesłu / pierwszemu / zwierzam / i jest wzruszenie / i
wspólne zgięcie / i teraz to ty / o krzesło / kocham cię / krzesło / kocham cię / i to jest miłość tragiczna / bo już jest / zaczajenie zdra-
dzonego oprócz krzesła / wypatrzy / wyjrzy mnie   będzie wyglądało
/ zemści się.

Such an uneasy, love- and fear-ridden relationship between man
and the objects surrounding him is encountered frequently in
Białoszewski's verse. Although objects may appear to offer a firm
anchor in reality, they are also wholly unreliable. The "I" of
Białoszewski's poems frequently appears to be under siege by the
malfunctioning, disintegrating, or obtrusive items and appliances
which are part of modern living.

III   *Fear and Withdrawal*

Fear of the larger world and a desire to retreat to some island of safety are frequent topics in Białoszewski's poems. These themes are most clearly developed in *Mylne wzruszenia* (Mistaken Emotions, 1961). The poems of the first section of this book, "Leżenia" ("Lyings-down"), appear to be the fruit of a serious emotional crisis in which the "I" is utterly incapacitated by its fear of leaving the haven of its warm bed, where it daydreams and writes. The poems of this cycle display an hypnotic, repetitive rhythm and a syntax which can only be described as childlike.[12] But even a regression to childlike helplessness amid the comforting warmth of his Mount Carmel quilt cannot provide sufficient protection; something threatening is always lurking nearby, awaiting its chance to attack even the most inoffensive of people:[13]

> such lying-down-thinking as I like
> is bad by nature
> because just let me
> lie-think like this in nature
> and something will immediately attack me and eat me up
>
> lying in bed I want to be good
> much goodness grows during sleep
> lying down warms up goodness
> but standing blows it away

takie leżenie-myślenie jak ja lubię / to jest niedobre z natury / bo niech ja w naturze / tak sobie leżę-myślę / to zaraz napadnie mnie coś i zje / / leżąc w łóżku chcę być dobrym / przez sen rośnie dużo dobroci / leżenie dobroć wygrzewa / ale wstanie ją zawiewa

By a curious twist of logic, what follows from this terror is that any encounter with the threatening outside world can be seen as an act of extreme bravery. Whatever happens in the world is considered significant, in part because it is potentially so menacing. An early poem, "A Ballad About Going Down to the Store," treats the theme of the valiant venture into the "real world" in the mock heroic style it deserves. But the humorous, self-deprecatory aspect of the presentation does not completely disguise the genuine underlying fear:[14]

> First I went down to the street
> by the stairs,
> ah, just imagine,
> by the stairs.
>
> Then acquaintances of nonacquaintances
> passed me, and I passed them.
> Feel sorry,
> that you did not see
> how the people were walking,
> feel sorry!
>
> I entered an honest-to-goodness store;
> lamps of glass were glowing,
> I saw someone who sat down,
> and what did I hear? . . . what did I hear?
> the sound of pocketbooks and human speech.
>
> Well then, really
> and truly
> I returned.

Najpierw zeszedłem na ulicę / schodami, / ach, wyobraźcie sobie, / schodami. / / Potem znajomi nieznajomych / mnie mijali, a ja ich. / Żałujcie, / żeście nie widzieli, / jak ludzie chodzą, / żałujcie! / / Wstąpiłem do zupełnego sklepu; / paliły się lampy ze szkła, / widziałem kogoś—kto usiadł, / i co słyszałem? . . . co słyszałem? / szum toreb i ludzkie mówienie. / / No naprawdę / naprawdę / wróciłem.

"A Ballad About Going Down to the Store" is interesting from several perspectives. In addition to its connection with Białoszewski's later theme of a paralyzing fear of the outside world, it is also obviously linked to other important aspects of his work. The first of these is a thoroughgoing iconoclasm which in *Revolutions of Things* (the volume in which "A Ballad" appears) frequently finds expression through an inappropriate use of genre. This iconoclasm has far-reaching results in Białoszewski's thorough modification of poetic language and traditional genre distinctions (see below, section IV). The easygoing humor of "A Ballad," in which the speaker is clearly aware of the ludicrous disjunction between his "feat" and his dramatic retelling of it, is an element of many of Białoszewski's poems. In fact, one of the most attractive features of his poetry is his light, sometimes flippant, humor, his refusal to take his own revolutionary pretensions too seriously. Finally, "A Ballad About Going Down to the Store" is a characteristic work because of the apparent triviality of its theme—a feature it shares with the majority of poems in *Mistaken Emotions*, part 2, and *It Was and It Was*, as well as with the prose collections.

In *Revolutions of Things* Białoszewski was concentrating on describing familiar items and revealing the hidden poetry within them. In *Mistaken Emotions* and *It Was and It Was* he shifted his emphasis from things to events. *Mistaken Emotions* contains two sections—"Lyings-Down" is followed by "Zajścia" ("Events"). In the second of these, the poet, as if pulling himself together by sheer willpower, leaves the asylum of his bed and returns to the world of the active. In most of the poems he is still basically passive himself, acting as a chronicler of events in which other people are the actors.

In *It Was and It Was* the "I" of the poem is more likely to be an actor. Poems from this collection include a number which are written as diary or "walk book" ("spacernik") entries. Among the "adventures" chronicled in these poems are accounts of train trips, descriptions of street scenes in which nothing in particular happens, reflections on Warsaw's history, reports of petty crimes. The anecdotes which these poems relate are a blend of that type of observation of city life often used as fillers in newspapers with a mixture of trivia and philosophizing such as is usually reserved for private diary jottings.[15]

Białoszewski's insistence on bringing into the realm of poetry experiences which normally are considered scarcely fit for lowbrow prose is most strikingly exemplified by the rather astonishing number of poems and prose fragments which deal with either excretory functions or plumbing. For example, in "From My Walk Book" he describes a vain search for a public urinal and his relief when he urinates against a city wall on Christmas Eve.[16] This poem provides a striking example of Białoszewski's inclination to defy the rules of social propriety and to mock unthinking reverence for tradition.

"Lu. He.'s Story" is typical of the humorous, inconsequential narratives which form the core of Białoszewski's late poetry and small prose pieces:[17]

> a long, long time ago, on Spokojna Street,
> the toilet got stuffed up,
> an expert was summoned, examined it,
> proclaimed:
>
> "too much paper!
> not enough water!
> too much paper!
> not enough water!"
>
> "What's to be done?"
>
> "less paper! more water!
> less paper! more water!"

dawno, dawno na Spokojnej / zapchało się w ubikacji, / zawołali rzeczoznawcę, zbadał, / orzekł: / / —za dużo papieru! / za mało wody! / za dużo papieru! / za mało wody! / / —a co robić? / / —mniej papieru! więcej wody! / mniej papieru! więcej wody!

The stuffed-up toilet and the "expert's" sage advice provide the kind of mild absurdity on which many of Białoszewski's anecdotes—both prose and verse—are based. "Lu. He.'s Story" is a serious poem, masquerading as a bit of nonpoetic buffoonery, about the individual's predicament in a world of faulty objects and know-nothing experts. But it is also a funny poem and should be accepted with the caveat Białoszewski has written into one of the stories in his latest prose collection: "It's ten o'clock ... night ... quiet, I go to vomit, I put on a record and now I'm going to write down .. all of this, all.... *Only people shouldn't take it all so seriously.*"[18]

In Białoszewski's poetry, ugliness and banality are not intended primarily as a means of shocking the reader or offending his sensibility. The aim of this poetry is, rather, to affirm life as it is. In all his work, Białoszewski, despite his revolutionary posture in terms of poetic technique, is essentially conservative: he is interested in being; never in becoming. In the poem "May 18 Continued" the poet contemplates the southern Warsaw skyline where the scattered church cupolas turn an otherwise ugly cityscape into an harmonious æsthetic whole. Questioning his emotional response to this view, Białoszewski discovers the following motivation for it:[19]

> . . . Mem-
> ories (?). Perhaps.
> With the result that I have moved on
> to the aesthetics of accepting
> everything. It wanted that
> itself. And perhaps it is being accepted. Like life.
> It is because it is.

. . . Wspo- / mnienia (?). / Może to / / Z tym, że ja przeszedłem / na estetykę przyjmowania / wszystkiego. Byleby tylko / przyjmować. Się chciało / samo. A chyba się przyjmuje. Jak to życie. / Jest bo jest.

IV *Questions of Style*

In terms of content alone, Białoszewski's poetry would appear to be exceedingly simple; what he deals with, after all, is the stuff of our daily existence. His poetry, however, is not at all easy. Its thematic ordinariness is itself an obstacle to easy comprehension because it is so different from what we expect to find as the subject matter of poetry. The major obstacle, however, to relatively easy comprehension of these poems lies in Białoszewski's use of language and his subversion of traditional poetic forms.[20] *Revolutions of Things*, Białoszewski's first volume, was still recognizably traditional, which is to say that he still paid rhyme, assonance, meter, and stanza patterns their due. In the succeeding three volumes, however, he has subjected poetic language and structure to radical innovations, the major goal of which has been to make poetry out of the lexicon and rhythms of the Warsaw man-in-the-street's spoken language.

In order to mimic the patterns of this spoken language, he uses a wide variety of linguistic and typographic stratagems.

They include: the use of local slang; the deliberate commission of grammatical errors such as are commonly made during speech; misspelling to indicate slurred pronunciation; peculiar punctuation as a visual substitute for inflectional emphasis and gesture; ellipses to imitate the silences and omissions so common in spoken language. This mimicry is further complicated by the use of neologisms, idiosyncratic usage, nonsense words, and private references which are obscure though linguistically clear.

Because of the wordplay involved in Białoszewski's poems, the most interesting among them are extremely difficult to translate. The following poem, "Hepyent (1)," may serve to give some idea of Białoszewski's linguistic maneuvers:[21]

> it's drizzlishing it's drizzlishing
> sleeping we hand we in hand dry ones
> we everything'sokayers
> ————————————————
> when earlybirds rise
> we still are passing the night
> ah oh ah the window dayishly dry
> clo. it!
> we still are passing the night

deszczyczkuje deszczyczkuje / śpiący my ręka my w rękę susi / dobrzenam'owie / —— / kiedy ranni wstają / jeszcze nocujemy / a o a okno dziennie suche / -zamk. je! / jeszcze nocujemy

Białoszewski's four published volumes of poetry demonstrate a consistent development away from the formal constraints of poetry in the direction of a very free prose style. Rhyme, assonance, meter, stanza forms, and metaphors are abandoned along the way, until, in his last volume, the main distinction between the works which he calls poetry and those which he labels prose seems to be the way in which the lines are set. In contemporary poetry the boundary between prose and verse is often blurred; thus it is a rare critic today who would claim that he could define with absolute precision where poetry ends and prose begins. Białoszewski's work is an extreme instance of this modern erosion of prose-poetry boundaries.

V   *Conclusion*

The culmination of Białoszewski's movement away from poetry—his masterful prose work, *A Memoir of the Warsaw Uprising*—is undeniably filled with "poetic" moments. This memoir and the two collections of prose narratives which followed illuminate retrospectively certain aspects of Białoszewski's poetics. The memoir shows the shattering impact on Białoszewski of the destruction of Warsaw. Although in his poetry Białoszewski, unlike Różewicz, rarely refers directly to the events of the occupation or the uprising, stylistically his poetry reflects the destructive force of his experiences. The fragmentation of language; the ungainly, clipped phrases; the emphasis on objects and discreet events—all are, at least in part, consequences of wartime experience. *A Memoir* makes obvious why objects can hold inexpressible terror for Białoszewski while, despite their treachery, they and the simple events of daily routines remain the focus of his poetry. During what he has called "the greatest experience of my life," they alone held some faint promise of survival.[22]

Białoszewski continues to perceive life as a composite of fragments which cannot be integrated into a meaningful larger whole. Indeed, only the individual's direct experience is considered meaningful knowledge. Reality, in Białoszewski's poetry, is a patchwork quilt of bits and pieces from ordinary life. The experience of the uprising taught Białoszewski how precious and how terribly ephemeral such fragments of daily routine can be.

The memory of World War II has begun to fade, but Białoszewski, like other writers of his generation, has been unable or unwilling to turn away from the truths that he perceived in the extremity of wartime. Białoszewski's poetry, like Różewicz's, is a kind of "antipoetry." Out of the devastation of his city Białoszewski has salvaged a poetics which sees beauty only in that which has been marginal to traditional poetic subject matter and finds its proper expression in a language which is the antithesis of the traditional well-turned, carefully organized line of verse. The roughness of Białoszewski's poetic fragments represents his vision of our world.

CHAPTER 8

Zbigniew Herbert:
In Defense of Civilization

ZBIGNIEW Herbert has some affinities with almost every one of the poets discussed here so far. Like Miłosz, he believes that high seriousness and a discursive style are not at all incompatible with poetic excellence. He views the question of the individual's responsibility to his nation as a matter of serious concern, as did Krzysztof Baczyński and Tadeusz Gajcy. Like other poet-survivors of the war generation (he is the youngest among them), he remains haunted by his sense of obligation to the dead. Herbert is a stern moralist, but his work lacks the presumption of moral superiority that can be detected in much of Różewicz's poetry. Like Białoszewski, he often writes about inanimate objects and sometimes about everyday events, but he is by no means obsessed with the commonplace. Herbert characteristically speaks in a dry ironic tone, one that is echoed in the best of Szymborska's work. Like Szymborska (and unlike Różewicz and Białoszewski) he does not feel that poetic language has been irreparably compromised by the barbarism of our century.

Herbert's language is an impeccable blend of literary and colloquial Polish. It is dignified and understated. In his exquisitely balanced poetry he confronts the central problems of contemporary Polish literature, gravely acknowledging man's limitations as citizen and artist, and displaying a sober respect for the tenacity of moral norms.

I. *Biographical Note*

Herbert was born in 1924 in the city of Lwów, which belonged to Poland during the two interwar decades. Located in what was then eastern Poland, in an area of mixed Ukrainian and Polish settlement, Lwów was annexed by the Soviet Union at the end of the war. Herbert's poetry reflects his loss of a living tie with his native city. Białoszewski and Harasymowicz, for example, are closely identified with Warsaw and Cracow, respectively; Miłosz, with the abstract state of exile (and latterly with America); Przyboś, with the Polish countryside; but Herbert's poetry has no location which can be called its own. Moreover, it generally lacks specific landscape descriptions.

Herbert has moved around more than many of his fellow poets. Only fifteen at the time of the German invasion, he soon joined an underground military unit. After the war, he studied economics, law, and philosophy, first in Cracow, then in the western city of Torun. He then settled in Warsaw, working at various white-collar jobs until he became a professional writer. From 1965 through 1971—years which saw a tightening of political controls over writers after the brief period of post-1956 liberalism—Herbert lived abroad in Europe and America (a one year's residence in California). He now makes his home once again in Poland.

Herbert began writing poetry as a teenager during the war. He published a few poems during the 1950s but did not make his formal debut as the author of a volume of poetry until 1956. He had preferred "to write for the drawer" and to wait until the times were propitious for the publication of his work as he wanted it to appear. His debut was impressive: one approximately seventy-five page book of poetry followed within a year by a volume almost twice as long. After this seeming explosion of productivity which actually represented a decade's work, Herbert slowed down his tempo of publication. During the two decades since his debut, he has published three new poetry collections, a slim volume of plays, and a collection of essays on European culture.[1] He has not published a new collection of verse since 1974, although individual poems have appeared in journals from time to time.

II *The Classical Heritage*

Herbert's first volume of poetry, *Struna światła* (A String of Light, 1956), reveals the assured hand of a mature poet. The basic theme of *A String of Light* is familiar: the postwar despair of a survivor seeking to salvage something of value from the shattered beliefs of the past. What is markedly different in Herbert's treatment of this theme is the assumption that the classical tradition remains a point of reference for the modern poet. There are numerous allusions in *A String of Light* to Greek and Roman myth. The past remains alive for Herbert as a rich source against which modern man can measure his own experiences of human tragedy.

The poem "To Apollo," for example, opens with a description of a statue of Apollo. The god is immersed completely in his own song, his lyre lifted up "to the heights of silence." This is Apollo as the poet envisioned him in his youth. The poet addresses the god, begging for the return of his youthful faith, but is answered in silence, for the god has been destroyed:[2]

> give me back my hope
> silent white head
> silence—
>   the neck is cracked
> silence—
>   the song has been cut off

oddaj moją nadzieję / milcząca biała głowo / / cisza— / pęknięta szyja / cisza— / złamany śpiew

The second part of the poem develops the contrast between the poetic possibilities dreamed of in youth and the realities of postwar existence. Contemplating the false legends of history, the poet measures his experience against impressions received from literature (presumably from *The Iliad*, not mentioned explicitly here, but the subject of several other poems by Herbert):

> the prophecies of poetry are false
> everything happened differently
> the fire of the poem was one thing
> the fire of the city was another
> Heroes did not return from their expedition
> There were no heroes

the undeserving survived
I am seeking a statue
immersed in my youth
there remains only an empty pedestal—
the trace of a hand seeking a form

mylne są wróżby poezji / wszystko było inaczej / inny był pożar poematu / inny był pożar miasta / Bohaterowie nie wrócili z wyprawy / Nie było bohaterów / ocaleli niegodni / szukam posągu / zatopionego w młodości / / pozostał tylko pusty cokoł— / ślad dłoni szukającej kształtu

"To Apollo" appears to echo Różewicz's cry of pain in "The Survivor" (see above, p. 76), but the two poets start from very different premises. The speaker in Różewicz's poem has to redefine basic moral concepts in the light of his wartime experience. Lost in a moral wilderness, he yearns for a master who will divide the world once again into simple categories of good and evil (light and darkness). Herbert's lyric speaker is more sophisticated, though his speech is as readily accessible (though not quite as elementary) as Różewicz's. He is concerned with ideas—specifically with the reliability of poetry. Like Różewicz's "I" he is aware that violence has been done to language and hence to poetry. His words speak of the strangulation of poetry but, and this is essential, his use of classical referents indicates that he still believes that the tradition is in some sense alive.

Repeatedly in *A String of Light,* as in his later collections of poetry, Herbert uses classical and other literary references as a measure of the present. In the earliest work he appears to be arguing that the relevance of the past has been all but eclipsed by the horror of the present. In "To Marcus Aurelius" the Stoic philosopher is said to be defeated by the onslaught of dark elemental terrors. The speaker in the poem summons the philosopher to strike back, for[3]

we shall be betrayed by the universe astronomy
calculations of the stars and wisdom of grass
by your too great eminence
and, Marcus, my helpless lament

zdradzi nas wszechświat astronomia / rachunek gwiazd i mądrość traw
/ i twoja wielkość zbyt ogromna / i mój bezradny Marku płacz

Although Herbert implicates philosophy and poetry in the
general betrayal of humanity, the poem in which he writes of
this casts doubt on his spoken rejection. "To Marcus Aurelius"
adheres closely, though not rigidly, to traditional poetic form.
(It is composed of three stanzas of eight lines each with a clear
tendency to iambic tetrameter. The stanzas have discernible,
but not rigid, patterns of alternating masculine and feminine
rhymes or assonances.) It is as if Herbert, having acknowledged
that poetry has been discredited, had made the pragmatic decision to use the tradition anyway, because there is no better
means of communicating the moral truths which concern him
most.

In his later works, Herbert uses classical literary references
in several ways. The living traditions to which they refer enable
him to move comfortably between the present and past. Historical and literary allusions allow Herbert to express in some
works political truths which cannot be stated directly. (See the
discussion of "The Elegy of Fortinbras" and "Return of the
Proconsul" below.) In other works they serve to emphasize the
terrible dullness of our own unheroic age. In "Jonah" Herbert
contrasts the biblical hero with his present-day counterpart.
In his cynical view, a latterday Jonah would refuse his destiny,
go into hiding to avoid sojourning in the belly of the whale,
and eventually die of cancer in some antiseptic hospital.[4]

Similarly, the prose poem "The Missing Knot" is a modern
variant of one of the great Greek tragic plots. In Herbert's ver-
sion, Agamemnon returns home from the wars to a complacent
Clytemnestra. Agisthos joins them to form a peaceful, theater-
going trio. Electra works in some kind of cooperative and Orestes,
who will soon marry, is a student of pharmacology.[5] There are
no complexes, no grudges, no feuds, no agony of soul-searching, no
evil destinies, and certainly no bloody murders. Everything is very
civil and very dull. But, as with Herbert's use of traditional
form for the vehicle by which he proclaims his disenchantment
with traditions, this type of debunking is a double-edged weapon. When the heroic past is used as a foil to underscore

the banality of the present, the glitter of that past is inevitably tarnished by association. Conversely, unprepossessing as it is, the present acquires some degree of grandeur when it is conceived of, even in reduced measure, as cut to a classical pattern. One can discern a certain kinship here with Jerzy Harasymowicz's and Miron Białoszewski's penchants for desanctification of treasured myths, but Herbert's use of this device is generally at a higher intellectual level.

III *Public Life and Moral Codes*

To say that Herbert's poetry in general is highly intellectual is not to assert that he functions in a rarefied atmosphere of literary and philosophical concerns. Certainly, these are areas of considerable importance to him, but he is also very much preoccupied in his poetry with the moral and practical implications of accommodation to existing social order. Some of the most savage attacks in contemporary poetry on the Polish heroic tradition can be found in Herbert's works. The prose poem "The Soldier," for example, is a caricature of the chivalrous Polish hero. Herbert's soldier sets out to war (the phrase used is "na wojenkę," a startling diminutive form which appears in perhaps the most popular of all Polish soldiers' songs), with a crimson scarf around his breast and three feathers in his cap. Crimson, of course, is Poland's color—also, the color of spilled blood. The three feathers (the number is magical) can be interpreted as representing the soldier's life force—his chances for a really dramatic use of his powers, akin to the three wishes in a fairy tale. The soldier squanders his first chance when he buys a peasant's horse "for a stout fist and one feather." He leaves his second feather with a young girl whom he has raped. Then he moves on:[6]

> At dawn he killed a soldier wearing an azure scarf. The fool had been sitting at the edge of the road like a hare on a boundary strip.
> Now that was real war. About a most important issue. Whether flags should be sewn from crimson or azure silk.
> Until once at a crossroads he noticed a bony old

woman. He doffed his cap and with sorrow noticed that
the third and final feather was slowly falling to the
ground.

O świcie zabił żołnierza z niebieską szarfą. Siedział głuptaś na skraju
drogi jak zając nad miedzą. / / To właśnie była wojna. O sprawę naj-
ważniejszą. Czy sztandary mają być szyte z purpurowego czy też z
niebieskiego jedwabiu. / / Aż raz na rozstaju zobaczył kościstą sta-
ruszkę. Zdjął kapelusz i z żalem zobaczył, że trzecie i ostatnie pióro
wolno opada na ziemię.

The satire of "The Soldier" is savage, but also deftly deployed.
The contrasts between elevated aspirations and tawdry deeds
are obvious. The one "heroic" deed, which does not cost a
feather, is a foolish squabble over national emblems. The "hero"
rapes the girl who might have been a symbol of victory and
loses his life ("the third feather") partly because he cannot for-
get his excellent manners before the old woman, death. (Death—
śmierć—is feminine in Polish.)

Herbert's disdain for the warrior myth does not lessen his grief
over the countless wartime dead. Even in the late 1960s Herbert
was still beset by his inability to resolve the competing claims
of the dead and the living—a theme which is already familiar
to us from the works of Miłosz and Różewicz. In "Five Men"
(from *Hermes, A Star and a Dog*), Herbert had argued that
men condemned to death are attached to the ordinary concerns
of life until their execution and that therefore a poet may, without guilt feelings, write about love and sunrises "and also / once
again / with mortal dignity / make the betrayed world an offering / of a rose" ("a także / jeszcze raz / ze śmiertelną powagą /
ofiarować zdradzonemu światu / różę").[7]

Herbert was not completely convinced of this himself, however. In the "Prologue" to *Napis* (Inscription, 1969) he dramatized the conflict within him as a dialogue between a poet
("He") and a chorus. "He" speaks from the narrow perspective
of personal experience, while the Chorus speaks from the broader
perspective of the ebb and flow of time in the natural order:[8]

Chorus:
Throw away keepsakes. Burn memories and enter the new
    stream of life,

There is only the earth. One earth and the seasons of the
    year are over it.
Wars of insects—wars of people and a brief death on a
    flower of honey.
The grain ripens. Oak trees bloom. Rivers descend from
    mountain to sea.

He:
I swim against the current and they are with me
implacably they look me in the eye
stubbornly they whisper old words
we eat our bitter bread of despair

I must carry them to a dry place
and build a large mound from sand
before spring buries them in flowers
and mighty green sleep stupefies them

Chór / Wyrzuć pamiątki. Spal wspomnienia i w nowy życia strumień
wstąp. / Jest tylko ziemia. Jedna ziemia i pory roku nad nią są. /
Wojny owadów—wojny ludzi i krótka śmierć nad miodu kwiatem. /
Dojrzewa zboże. Kwitną dęby. W ocean schodzą rzeki z gór. / / On /
Płynę pod prąd a oni ze mną / nieubłaganie patrzą w oczy / uparcie
szepczą słowa stare / jemy nasz gorzki chleb rozpaczy / / Muszę ich
zawieść w suche miejsce / i kopczyk z piasku zrobić duży / zanim im
wiosna sypnie kwiaty / i mocny zielny sen odurzy

There is no real solution to this difficulty. The poet can only
lament that fate has burdened him with love for such a troubled
fatherland.

As with Miłosz, Herbert's sometimes reluctant sense of responsibility to the dead is paralleled by ambivalent feelings
about his Polishness. Nonetheless, he has adopted as a fundamental moral position a thoughtful allegiance to the nation.
Herbert's poems on public themes reveal both his closeness to
Czesław Miłosz and the fundamental difference between their
situations. Herbert, like Miłosz, is concerned with the morality
of political actions and inaction. He is coolly intellectual, trans-
forming his moral outrage into irony. But he does not speak
with the blunt fury of Miłosz's poems of the 1950s. Because he
has not chosen to emigrate (although his many years abroad

appear to indicate how serious a temptation this option is for
him), nor to evade the censorship by publishing abroad (as
writers such as Jerzy Andrzejewski have done on occasion),
Herbert's poems must always meet the rules of Polish censorship.
His approach to political themes has had to be more subtle than
Miłosz's once was and, it must be conceded, his poetry on public
themes gains from these constraints.

Some of Herbert's finest poems focus on the problem of acting
as a public person in a political arena which provides only a
minimal freedom ˙of choice. "Return of the Proconsul" alludes
to Roman history but is clearly directed at problems of the
present. The speaker of the poem has gone into voluntary re-
tirement to evade the unpleasant duties foisted upon members
of the tyrant's inner circle. In an interior monologue, the proconsul, seeking to bolster his courage and to quell his doubts
about the propriety of his plans, reviews the case for returning
to the emperor's court. He assures himself that he can easily
find a degree of accommodation which will protect both his
life and the purity of his conscience. Although his qualms are
of a moral order, his thoughts inevitably focus on the details of
survival by cunning. He elaborates a plan of facial control to
conceal his inner thoughts and a strategy of evasive action to
avoid drinking with the emperor (thus protecting himself simultaneously from moral contamination and physical poisoning).

Herbert's presentation of the proconsul's ruminations is
masterful. Without any third-person commentary, he allows
the proconsul to convict himself with his own arguments. The
proconsul's words of assurance about the tyrant's humanity are
actually damning, and his stout prediction of success is belied
by the quavering final two lines of the poem. This is achieved
in a taut free-verse style, in which the lines of verse correspond
to measured spoken phrases, and the lame ending speaks as
resoundingly as the most polished rhetoric:[9]

> Of one thing I am sure I will not drink wine with him
> when he brings his goblet nearer I will lower my eyes
> and pretend I'm picking bits of food from between my teeth
> besides the emperor likes courage of convictions
> to a certain extent to a certain reasonable extent

he is after all a man like everyone else
and already tired by all those tricks with poison

. . . .
I've decided to return to the emperor's court
Yes I hope that things will work out somehow

jednego jestem pewien wina z nim pić nie będę / kiedy zbliża swój
kubek spuszczę oczy / i będę udawał że z zębów wyciągam resztki je-
dzenia / cesarz lubi odwagę cywilną / do pewnych granic do pewnych
rozsądnych granic / to w gruncie rzeczy człowiek tak jak wszyscy / i
już bardzo zmęczony sztuczkami z trucizną / . . . / / Postanowiłem
wrócić na dwór cesarza / mam naprawdę nadzieję że jakoś to się
ułoży

In his well-known "Elegy of Fortinbras"—which follows directly after "Return of the Proconsul" in *Studium przedmiotu*
(Study of the Object, 1961)—Herbert continues his weighing
of the costs and achievements of idealism versus those of pragmatism. Here victorious Fortinbras addresses Hamlet's corpse,
mocking the prince's impractical idealism, his foolish softness
which made his early death inevitable. The time is ripe for a
man of action to stand at the helm, Fortinbras declares:[10]

Now you have peace Hamlet you did what it was your task to do
and you have peace The rest is not silence but belongs to me
you chose the easier part a dramatic thrust
but what is a hero's death compared to eternal vigilance
with a cold apple in one's hand on a high throne
with a view of the antheap and the face of the clock

Adieu prince a sewer project awaits me
and a decree on prostitutes and beggars
I must also elaborate a better system of prisons
for as you justly observed Denmark is a prison
I go to my duties This night is born
a star Hamlet We shall never meet
what remains after me will not be the subject of a tragedy

It.is not for us to greet each other to bid farewell we live on
 archipelagos

and this water these words what can they do prince what can
they do

Teraz masz spokój Hamlecie zrobiłeś co do ciebie należało / i masz
spokój Reszta nie jest milczeniem ale należy do mnie / wybrałeś część
łatwiejszą efektowny sztych / lecz czymże jest śmierć bohaterska wo-
bec wiecznego czuwania / z zimnym jabłkiem w dłoni na wysokim
krześle / z widokiem na mrowisko i tarczę zegara / / Żegnaj książę
czeka na mnie projekt kanalizacji / i dekret w sprawie prostytutek i
żebraków / muszę także obmyślić lepszy system więzień / gdyż jak
zauważyłeś słusznie Dania jest więzieniem / Odchodzę do moich spraw
Dziś w nocy urodzi się / gwiazda Hamlet / Nigdy się nie spotkamy /
to co po mnie zostanie nie będzie przedmiotem tragedii / / Ani nam
witać się ani żegnać żyjemy na archipelagach / a ta woda te słowa
cóż mogą cóż mogą książę

"Elegy of Fortinbras" demonstrates Herbert's sophisticated
use of restrained irony. As in "Return of the Proconsul," Herbert
refrains here from any overt interference in the poem, preferring
to create an ironic distancing effect by allowing the speaker's
words to tell against him. Fortinbras's poetic diction is imposing.
He speaks in succinct phrases set in verse lines whose measured
dignity and length are an effective reminiscence of Shakespeare's
blank verse. A few phrases are borrowed from *Hamlet* but subjected to Fortinbras's interpretation. Intellectually, Fortinbras's
argument is irrefutable: dreamers who ignore the basic functions
of government do not make good rulers. But Fortinbras betrays
himself and his professed indignation by his goal of improving
the prison system which is Denmark. Herbert has thus confronted us with a Hobson's choice: for he has let Fortinbras
convince us simultaneously of Hamlet's futility and his own evil.

The relevance of "Elegy of Fortinbras" to the Polish political
situation is obvious. Polish readers, long attuned to "Aesopian
language," would immediately understand that in Poland, as in
Hamlet's Denmark, the practical reformers would not be idealists,
and their improvements in the prison system of the state would
be undertaken for their own, not the public's, ends. The political
implications to be drawn from this insight are not at all clear,
however, for it is not Herbert's purpose to sketch a political
program. He is a poet whose verse is born in the controversies of

his age; he is not, and this must be stressed, a political pamphleteer masquerading as a poet. By his own definition, Herbert is a moralist whose poetry emits a sharp, crackling "yes" or "no."[11] But "Elegy of Fortinbras" demonstrates that there are few occasions for which such clarity is appropriate. This is the ethical message of many of Herbert's poems and prose poems; it is the source of his characteristic irony. Like Różewicz, Herbert is a moralist; unlike Różewicz, he never moralizes. Because his irony is subtle and controlled, the best of his poems on contemporary issues have a far greater resonance than do Różewicz's poems on similar themes, in which the poet's angry voice leaves little room for the reader to create his own responses.

IV   *Stones and Empty Spaces*

The related questions of what is worthy of aesthetic contemplation and how one can achieve unclouded perception are major themes in Herbert's poetry. In Herbert's work, as in that of others among his contemporaries, such as Białoszewski and Harasymowicz, there is a fascination with inanimate objects as more constant and more revealing of essential truths than are human beings. People distort and conceal their true nature, often to the point of annihilating what lies at the core. Objects may suffer deformation and destruction, but they do not conceal or manipulate their own selves or others. Tangible objects are viewed by Herbert as touchstones; their steadfastness is an implied rebuke to human falsity, but their existence is also somehow a proof of our existence. If we can perceive and value the immutability of objects, Herbert seems to argue, then we may come to some understanding of our modest place in a limitless universe.

There appear to be two classes of objects in Herbert's world: those which are functional and those which hold themselves aloof from human need. On the first Herbert bestows his bemused condescension: tables are patient gray donkeys with wrinkled skin scarred by wet glasses,[12] and chairs are the servile descendants of once-beautiful quadrupeds, whose creaking expresses their despair.[13] In general, contact with people is felt to be demeaning for objects. This is expressed humorously in Herbert's short prose piece, "The Hen." The main point of "The Hen" is a pointed jibe

at sycophantic poets (Herbert is outspoken in his contempt for
poetasters, translators, and literary critics), but the first lines of
the work clearly demonstrate in passing his dislike for anything
which has been domesticated to serve human wants:[14]

> The hen is the best example of what intimacy with
> people leads to. It has completely lost any birdlike light-
> ness and grace. Its tail protrudes over its prominent
> rump like an oversized hat in bad taste. Its rare moments
> of ecstasy, when it stands on one leg and glues together
> its rounded eyes with their filmy lids, are shockingly
> loathsome. And to top it off, that parody of song, its
> strangled supplications over an unspeakably ridiculous
> object: a rounded, white, smeared egg.
> The hen reminds one of certain poets.

> Kura jest najlepszym przykładem, do czego doprowadza bliskie
> współżycie z ludźmi. Zatraciła zupełnie ptasią lekkość i wdzięk. Ogon
> sterczy nad wydatnym kuprem jak za duży kapelusz w złym guście.
> Jej rzadkie chwile uniesienia, kiedy staje na jednej nodze i zakleja
> okrągłe oczy błoniastymi powiekami, są wstrząsająco obrzydliwe. I w
> dodatku to parodia śpiewu, poderżnięte suplikacje nad rzeczą niewy-
> powiedzianie śmieszne: okrągłym, białym, umazanym jajkiem.
> Kura przypomina niektórych poetów.

The second class of objects, those which do not lend themselves
to human exploitation (except, perhaps, by artists), represents for
Herbert an approximation of perfection. The epitome of such
objects is a stone. In "Pebble" Herbert describes this perfection as
an object being what it is and only what it is. The pebble is self-
contained; it has no odor, shape, or color that might arouse
association with anything else. It is essentially nonfunctional and
appears to assert its independent "pebbleness." The poet confesses to a feeling of discomfort when his human presence intrudes
upon the stony existence of a pebble:[15]

> I feel a heavy remorse
> when I hold it in my hand
> and its noble body
> is permeated by false warmth

Pebbles cannot be tamed
to the end they will look at us
with a calm and very clear eye

czuję ciężki wyrzut / kiedy go trzymam w dłoni / i ciało jego szla-
chetne / przenika fałszywe ciepło / / —Kamyki nie dają się oswoić / do
końca będą na nas patrzeć / okiem spokojnym bardzo jasnym

"Pebble" raises a profoundly important question. Clearly, to
write about or portray the perfection which the pebble symbol-
izes is to diminish that perfection, to impart to it the false warmth
of a human hand. The implied alternative is silence—the blank
page or canvas. But the artist or writer is what he is precisely
because he is driven to inscribe something on the blankness. So,
although the perfect response may be silence, in practice the
artist is faced with the pragmatic problem of finding the least
deforming way of perceiving and representing the world.

Herbert asserts that a basic choice must be made between
rational and intuitive perception. Despite the high value he places
on rationality, he declares himself firmly in favor of intuition. His
most significant elaboration of this theme is "A Study of the
Object," which draws together the related problems of manner
and matter of perception. The most beautiful object, Herbert
affirms here, is one which does not exist, which has no function,
shape, texture, or term of existence. Herbert suggests that the
appropriate way to honor this nonexistent object is to frame its
absence in a black square (as in a necrology? or a modern geometrical canvas?). This square will cause an aesthetic eruption
so great that the square itself will be annihilated and pure empty
space, "more beautiful than the object / more beautiful than the
space it occupied," will be created. This is true creativity—the
opening of perception to vision by the inner eye.

Herbert warns us that the intellect will find itself bombarded
by realistic images which the material world will offer, but that
the artist must firmly defend his inner vision. The concluding
section of this six-part poem presents such an inner vision in
which the artist's perception transforms an item of common
reality into an object of aesthetic purity which intellect alone
could not comprehend:[16]

extract
from the shadow of the object
which does not exist
from polar space
from the stern reveries of the inner eye
a chair

beautiful and useless
like a cathedral in the wilderness

place on the chair
a crumpled tablecloth
add to the idea of order
the idea of adventure

let it be a confession of faith
before the vertical struggling with the horizontal

let it be
quieter than angels
prouder than kings
more substantial than a whale
let it have the face of the last things

    we ask reveal oh chair
    the depths of the inner eye
    the iris of necessity
    the pupil of death

wyjmij / z cienia przedmiotu / którego nie ma / z polarnej przestrzeni / z surowych marzeń wewnętrznego oka / krzesło / / piękne i bezużyteczne / jak katedra w puszczy / / połóż na krześle / zmiętą serwetę / dodaj do idei porządku / ideę przygody / / niech będzie / cichsze od aniołów / dumniejsze od królów / prawdziwsze niż wieloryb / niech ma oblicze rzeczy ostatecznych / / prosimy wypowiedz o krzesło / dno wewnętrznego oka / tęczówkę konieczności / źrenicę śmierci

For Herbert, then, when he wrote his "Study of the Object," the pursuit of inner vision, in which the object perceived is less important than the aura surrounding it in the beholder's subjective perception, led directly to a kind of Oriental mysticism. This could not have been a comfortable position for a poet in a communist country where, officially at least, realism is still considered the highest form of art. With Herbert, more than with most other Polish poets, one feels that blunt as his poetry is, there is still very much of significance that he leaves unsaid.

V   *Mr. Cogito*

The moment of epiphany achieved in "Study of the Object" is not something which can easily be repeated. But one can find in Herbert's latest volume of poems, *Pan Cogito* (Mr. Cogito, 1974), the working out in practice of this intense awareness that the ordinary may provide the key to metaphysical mystery. Mr. Cogito, the guiding consciousness in these poems, is a kind of intellectual everyman (if such a creature can be imagined). He is clearly a descendant of Valéry's cerebral, analytical persona, M. Teste. At sea in the moral wilderness of the twentieth century, he worries about his own responsibility. His meditations touch on universal themes: the threatening father of childhood metamorphosed in old age into a fragile child; the inevitability of suffering; the lost shelter of a mother's arms.

Mr. Cogito reads the newspapers, turns to philosophy, literature, and religion for help, and finds it nowhere. Science, he concludes, has done no better than the humanities. By training its sights on erudite questions it has avoided the simplest and yet most difficult of them all: how is man to live?[17]

> So many dictionaries
> obese encyclopedias
> but no one to give advice
>
> they explored the sun
> the moon the stars
> they lost me
>
> . . . .
>
> Perhaps Rabbi Nachman
> could give me advice
> but how can I find him
> among so many ashes

Tyle książek słowników / opasłe encyklopedie / ale nie ma kto porad-
zić / / zbadano słońce / księżyc gwiazdy / zgubiono mnie / / . . .
/ / może by mi poradził / rabi Nachman / ale jak mam go znaleźć /
wśród tylu popiołów

The simple directness of these lines is typical of the poems in
Mr. Cogito. Herbert is concerned here with the most important
of moral issues and is at pains to keep his verse transparent. The
stark lines have the strength and beauty of clarity; stylistic
flourishes would be obtrusive.

Mr. Cogito has the yearnings of a hero; he is a would-be St.
George deprived by his times of a tangible monster against which
to test his strength. Evil in this day is formless, intangible, and
Mr. Cogito can only hope that he will find an opportunity to take
his moral stand:[18]

> Lucky Saint George
> from his knight's saddle
> could exactly evaluate
> the strength and movements
> of the enemy
>
> the first principle of strategy
> is to assess the opponent
>
> Mr. Cogito
> is in a worse position
>
> he sits
> in the low saddle of a valley
> covered with thick fog
>
> through fog you do not see
> glittering eyes
> an open jaw
>
> through fog you see only
> the shimmering of nothingness
>
> the monster of Mr. Cogito
> doesn't really have measurements

it is spread out like low pressure
hanging over the country

you can't touch it
with a pen
or with a spear

were it not for its suffocating weight
and the death it sends down
one would think
it is an abstraction
of the type *informel*

. . . . . .

the proof of the existence of the monster
is its victims
it is not direct proof
but sufficient

Szczęśliwy święty Jerzy / z rycerskiego siodła / mógł trafnie ocenić /
siły i ruchy wroga / / pierwsza zasada strategii / szacunek przeciwnika
/ / Pan Cogito / jest w gorszym położeniu / / siedzi / w niskim siodle
doliny / zasnutej gęstą mgłą / / przez mgłę nie widać / oczu błysz-
czących / paszczy otwartej / / przez mgłę widać tylko / migotanie
nicości / / potwór Pana Cogito / nie ma właściwie wymiarów / / jest
jak rozległy niż / wiszący nad krajem / / nie można go dotknąć / ani
piórem / ani włocznią / / gdyby nie duszny ciężar / i śmierć którą
zsyła / można by sądzić / że jest abstrakcją / z rodzaju informel / /
. . . / / dowodem istnienia potwora / są jego ofiary / jest to dowód nie
wprost / ale wystarczający

Unable to do battle with an evil opponent which has no form
and acknowledges no challenger, Mr. Cogito to retain his self-
respect must go through life making at least the gestures of
opposition, hoping that before his "ordinary death without glory /
suffocation from formlessness," he will have provoked shapeless
fate into a head-on encounter. Out of Mr. Cogito's yearnings, his
pain, his human weaknesses, Herbert finally derives a moment of
inspiration in which the moral ideal of humanity is revealed. "The
Envoy of Mr. Cogito," which concludes this volume of poems,
is resonant with unyielding moral fervor:[19]

you were saved not in order to live
you have little time you must give testimony

. . . .
and do not forgive truly it is not in your power
to forgive in the name of those betrayed at dawn

beware however of unnecessary pride
keep looking at your clown's face in the mirror
repeat: I was called—weren't there better ones than I

. . . .
repeat old incantations of humanity fables and legends
because this is how you will attain the good you will not attain
repeat great words repeat them stubbornly
like those crossing the desert who perished in the sand

. . . .
Be faithful Go

ocalałeś nie po to aby żyć / masz mało czasu trzeba dać świadectwo
/ / . . . / / i nie przebaczaj zaiste nie w twojej mocy / przebaczać w
imieniu tych którzy zdradzono o świcie / / strzeż się jednak dumy
niepotrzebnej / oglądaj w lustrze swą błazeńską twarz / powtarzaj:
zostałem powołany—czyż nie było lepszych / / . . . / / powtarzaj stare
zaklęcia ludzkości bajki i legendy / bo tak zdobędziesz dobro którego
nie zdobędziesz / powtarzaj wielkie słowa powtarzaj je z uporem / jak
ci co szli przez pustynię i ginęli w piasku / / . . . / / Bądź wierny Idź

This resounding summons to virtue, with its strong echoes of
Miłosz's poems of moral striving, is Herbert's last important poetic
statement to appear in print as of this writing.

VI *Conclusion*

Zbigniew Herbert is a poet-moralist whose insistence on moral
perfection coexists with an unblinking acceptance of human im-
perfection. Unlike other members of the generation of the 1920s—
Różewicz and Białoszewski in particular—he does not feel that
the experiences of World War II have proved the bankruptcy of
literary traditions. The past of legend, history, and literature is

alive for him, and he uses it effectively to lend resonance to his ironic observations on the human condition.

His poetry is modern in that he uses free verse and a blend of colloquial and literary language, but it is "classical" in the degree to which it is marked by intellectual clarity. His emotions are tightly controlled, rarely yielding to pathos or outrage. With his sharp ironic wit, he creates crystalline poetry out of the pained existence of poets, politicians, and ordinary men.

CHAPTER 9

Jerzy Harasymowicz: Retreat Into Fantasy

JERZY Harasymowicz is a strikingly eccentric poet. Not only does he hold himself aloof from contemporary literary movements but he appears to be at odds even with himself. The more than twenty volumes of poetry he has published since his debut in 1956 show him frequently shifting or reversing directions. His radical changes of theme and mood appear to be the product of spiritual deracination rather than a positive sign of continuous development. With an apparent lack of discrimination, Harasymowicz publishes poems of high imaginative and emotive power together with verse which seems scarcely more than self-parody. His abdication of an author's right to conceal his weaknesses through self-censorship (during his lifetime, at least) makes any assessment of his talents and significance in contemporary Polish poetry rather difficult. Critical estin.ates of Harasymowicz's talent have varied widely, but he has never lacked popular appeal and his books appear in unusually large editions.[1]

I *Allegiances*

Jerzy Harasymowicz was born in the town of Puławy in central Poland in 1933. He now lives in Cracow and considers himself an adopted native of that historic city and the Carpathian regions to the south along the Polish-Czech border. He has had professional experience as a land surveyor and forester.

The Polish traditions which inspire Harasymowicz are embodied in the medieval and baroque architecture of Cracow's churches and its Wawel Castle. He feels a deep attraction to quaint wooden shrines and religious statuary—the remnants of a now moribund folk culture from the mountain regions where

138

Poles, Ukrainians, and Slovaks once mixed their languages and religious practices. With few exceptions, the locale of Harasymowicz's poetry, the focal point of his abundant imagery, is the narrowly delimited region from Cracow south to the Tatra foothills, which he has staked out as his private poetic realm. In a sense, Harasymowicz is to Cracow and its environs what Białoszewski is to Warsaw and its outskirts. The latter poet draws from his locale, with its violently dislocated past, his dominant theme of the fragmentation of urban existence. The former finds in his economically more backward region, which was also spared the physical destruction visited upon Warsaw during the war, the important theme of a living tradition and its clash with intrusive modernity.

II Stylistic Features of Harasymowicz's Verse

Although Harasymowicz's poetry ranges among widely divergent themes, a number of shared stylistic features can be identified as bearing his poetic signature. As a rule, his verse line is extremely short, seldom exceeding eight syllables. Harasymowicz frequently uses rhyme or assonance—devices which impart to his poetry a slightly old-fashioned flavor. His longer poems tend to be divided into loosely structured quatrains. His vocabulary is not erudite, but is marked by frequent references to specific birds, plants and animals and the occasional use of archaisms, regionalisms and slang.

The rhythmic structure of Harasymowicz's poetry is uninteresting as a rule, in part because of the brevity of his verse line. But what his verse lacks in musicality is more than compensated for by richness of imagery. Indeed, the distinguishing feature of Harasymowicz's style is the inventiveness and abundance of his extravagant metaphors, which link the real and fantastic worlds, the world of man and the world of nature. Some of his metaphors are repeated so insistently that they become simply symbols or even emblems (e.g., his substitution of a wooden writing table for the flying horse Pegasus as a symbol of poetic inspiration). More frequently, the imagery is elaborate and unexpected as, for example, the description of a sunset as a group of red squirrels who have settled on the bronze cupola of an orthodox church in

the mistaken belief that it is a nut.[2] He has described heavy-
uddered cows as the devil's wives whose milk is sought by a
meek God in a chef's hat,[3] and has turned an ordinary ironing
board into the tablets which Moses brought down from Mount
Sinai.[4]

The comparison of one aspect of nature to another and the
association through metaphor of widely divergent spheres of
existence are both characteristic of Harasymowicz's use of poetic
imagery. Often, the metaphors he creates engender their own
poetic reality, while the original elements of the comparison are
abandoned to a prosaic limbo. Harasymowicz relies on the emotive
value of imagery, rather than on rational discourse, as his prime
means of communication.

Thematically, Harasymowicz's poetic work can be divided
into five main categories: (1) sentimental and idyllic evocations
of nature in the southern Polish countryside; (2) fantasies which
derive from the religious folk art of this region; (3) fantasies of
a grotesque and brutal nature; (4) poems on the city of Cracow,
as the embodiment of Poland's legendary past and the seat of her
contemporary proletarian bohemia (which may itself be a fantasy); (5) poems on poetry and the poet's inner needs. Although
all these themes may be found at various stages of Harasymowicz's
writing career, they have been listed here in the temporal order
in which they have become prominent.

III   *Homage to Nature*

Harasymowicz's first book appeared in 1956—a year of poetic
bounty in Poland. Bearing the title *Cuda* (Miracles), it is a wide-
eyed, childlike celebration of the world of nature, depicted with
the simplicity of a fairy-tale world or a medieval tapestry in which
animals live innocently in a garden of perpetual delight. In the
charming poem "The Garden, January" the whiteness of the
winter landscape is highlighted by red-breasted bullfinches,
whom the poet depicts as apples with a living heart as their core.
The only element of fear which disturbs the idyllic nature of the
winter garden is the white owl of the January night, but it is not
particularly menacing.[5]

The delightful innocence of *Miracles* verges at times on sentimentality—a danger which frequently threatens Harasymowicz's work. In "The Age of Innocence," for example, a child is seen through a golden haze, a "little angel" who breaks off a sunflower's head and learns the painful lesson that beauty is all too easily destroyed:[6] "The twilight's deliberations are ending, / and that head, now it's fallen, is fallen" ("Już zmierzchów się kończy narada, / a ta głowa jak spada, tak spada"). The repetitions and the use of ternary meter in these lines are meant presumably to justify, by their echo of folk ditties, the excessive sweetness of the vision.

Miracles contains a prose self-portrait in which Harasymowicz projects the first of the many personae he has adopted in his poetic career. In this work, "Authentic Portrait of the Author," the poet appears as a spirit of the forest, battling against the literary establishment. His heart, he asserts, is a naive chick and his banner a green flag of laziness stretching toward the sky.[7] As we shall see, Harasymowicz does not always fly the verdant flag of nature, but, in a variety of guises, he constantly poses as an outsider and opponent of the representatives of official culture. His rebellion, however, is almost always fanciful and harmless.

Harasymowicz's homage to nature is not that of a romantic. The natural landscape which he describes or, more accurately, transforms through his metaphors, is not the majestic landscape of mountains, waterfalls, and imposing forests so dear to the romantic soul, but the humbler scenery of a piedmont region.[8] Harasymowicz's affection for the familiar rather than the dramatic elements of the natural world has drawn him to descriptions of the sleepy provincial towns and villages nestled in these foothills. Usually he portrays himself as the sole inhabitant of his landscapes. When another man appears in the poems on the Carpathian foothills, he is likely to be a lone peasant (if he is real) or, more often, a weather-beaten wooden saint with a human spirit.

In the best of Harasymowicz's poems on the subcarpathian district a discreet merging of the human and animal worlds is achieved through a series of unusual images. "Little Carpathian Town" offers a striking example of the poet's method of composing a verbal painting through image sequences:[9]

. . . At one end a skinny John the Baptist shuns the sin of
    avarice,
so he drives the fat hens from his chapel to flutter above
    the town.
Opposite, beneath the red sail of his nose, Saint Florian
has the golden boat of his moustache like a half moon, and
    is separated by a low fence from the tulips' flames.

. . . Na jednym końcu Jan Chrzciciel chudziutki nie chce łakomstwem
zgrzeszyć, / więc tłuste kury z swej kaplicy wygania, aż trzepocą nad
miasteczkiem. / Naprzeciw św. Florian, pod nosa czerwonym żaglem /
ma jak półksiężyc złotą łódkę wąsów, i od ognia tulipanów jest ogrod-
zony płoteczkiem.

The domesticated Saints John and Florian in this poem are an
early manifestation of Harasymowicz's treatment of folk religious
statuary.

Harasymowicz's later nature poems tend to be less serene and
more complicated than those in *Miracles* or *Powrót do kraju
łagodności* (Return to the Land of Gentleness, 1958). The poetic
"I" drops its worshipful attitude. Harasymowicz becomes pro-
gressively more conscious of the writer's role in creating that
which he describes; in effect, he begins to vie with God for the
title of Creator. In the title poem of *Znaki nad domem* (Signs Over
the House, 1971), a poem in seven sections which are subdivided
into loosely rhymed quatrains, virtually every quatrain contains
at least one image which emphasizes nature's energy. The following verses exemplify Harasymowicz's penchant for describing
natural phenomena from an animistic perspective. The onset of
a mountain storm is being dramatized:[10]

In the heat a cuckoo summons
From ancient larches their larcher soul
And a storm is rolled in from over Slovakia
As treetrunks are rolled through a storehouse

The poppies whirl about
And the poppies seethe with excitement
As the heart does at times
When there are too many poems within it

And it thunders as if the mountain god
Were showering plums on the Ruthenian church
And the windstorm shakes loose from the pear trees
All of the old man's greed.

I wywołuje kukułka w upale / Z modrzewi starych modrzewiową duszę
/ I jakby przetaczali pnie na składzie / Przetoczyli znad Słowacji burzę
/ / I maki bardzo się kłębią / I maki bardzo się burzą / Jak serce kiedy
czasem / Wierszy w sercu za dużo / / I grzmi jakby sypał śliwy / Do
ruskiej cerkwi górski bóg / I całą chciwość dziadka / Wytrząsa wichura
z grusz.

In this poem, as in others, the various realms of God, nature,
man, and poetry are presented as virtually indivisible.

Signs Over the House, written some fifteen years after *Miracles,*
is a work of far greater aesthetic and philosophical complexity.
Whereas the earlier volume is marked by a certain smug com-
placency, the later book demonstrates a decided absence of
spiritual security. Harasymowicz confesses that immersion in
nature provides an insufficient guarantee of spiritual peace. In
"Bad Weather in the Mountains," the last poem of *Signs Over
the House,* Harasymowicz admits that what he sees in nature
now is the dreary landscape of his own troubled soul: "There's
bad weather / Both in body and soul" ("Jest niepogoda / Ciała
i duszy").[11] His new self-portrait is a ragged old man fighting
off a swarm of mosquitoes, a lifetime removed from the wide-
eyed youngster in the dreamworld of his earliest work. He is
aware by now that a natural paradise is a figment of the imagination. In reality the gentle cows go unmilked and the little
Ruthenian church (whose presence in the poem gives the landscape its regional identity) is like a coffin. Faced with this sad
emptiness, which is a stark reversal of the gay and impish imagery
of *Miracles* and *Return to the Land of Gentleness,* the poet now
declares that the adornments he has celebrated in God's world
have actually been of his own creation:

> I stripped from myself
> The shirt of my verse
> I covered God
> And the cupola

For always homeless
In His house
I used to write
With a golden flagstaff.

Ściągnąłem z siebie / Wiersza koszulę / Nakryłem Boga / I tę kop-
ułę / / Bo w jego domu / Zawsze bezdomny / Pisałem złotym / Drzew-
cem chorągwi.

IV   *Homely Saints and Careworn Madonnas*

A subject which parallels the theme of nature in Harasymowicz's poetry and which is intimately related to the Carpathian
landscape is the religious folk art of this region. Harasymowicz
writes extensively about church decorations, religious pictures,
and wooden statuary. The figures of saints, madonnas, and
suffering Christs serve as catalysts for the poet's imagination.
The local saints and madonnas substitute in his poetic world for
the living rural population which is conspicuous by its absence.

Although individual poems on religious figures can be found
in almost every volume of Harasymowicz's verse, *Mit o świętym
Jerzym* (The Myth of Saint George, 1959), *Podsumowanie zieleni*
(Summation of Green, 1964), *Pastorałki polskie* (Polish Pastorals,
1964), and *Madonny polskie* (Polish Madonnas, 1969) are especially rich in their development of this theme. In the earliest
of these volumes, *The Myth of Saint George*, the title poem is
illustrative of the desanctification which characterizes Harasymowicz's approach to religious motifs. St. George is turned from a
saint into a peasant, his banner serves as a pillow tick, his armor
is converted into roofing material, and his fire-breathing dragon
is metamorphosed whimsically into a sulphur-belching cow.[12]
(It is not unimportant that the deflated St. George is the poet's
patron saint.)

Harasymowicz's most original treatment of the folk-religion
motif is *Polish Madonnas*, which includes fourteen poems on as
many different wooden madonnas. All these poems follow essentially the same pattern: the poet expresses his admiration
for a particular madonna either in descriptive narrative addressed to the reader or in a laudatory apostrophe addressed

to the madonna. The madonna also speaks, answering the poet's questions and expressing her own concerns. The balance between narrative descriptive elements and dialogue varies from poem to poem.[13] The madonnas' speech is laced with regional dialect and feminine usage (more diminutives and endearing terms), while the poet's is a firmer, masculine, literary Polish. Each of these madonnas emerges as an individual woman, distinctive not only in sculptural detail but in personality as well.

The madonna in "Pieta from Znamierowice," for example, worries about her appearance, while feeling guilty because she cares about the condition of her crown when her poor son's little wooden legs and arms are broken.[14] The "City Madonna with Infant—The One Without a Crown" complains about her sister madonna who dresses in fancy clothing and jewels, while she is charged with all the housekeeping.[15] In "Madonna near Barcice" the poet begins by expressing his surprise at coming upon this unknown madonna who is not listed in his guide books. He praises her good looks, her round face, and noble air. Her response has the simplicity and directness of a folk song:[16]

> That's only
> our beauty
> that's our Carpathian
> style
> trouble never
> shows on us.

Taka już / nasza uroda / taka podkarpacka / moda / na nas nigdy / nie znać biedy.

The poem ends with the madonna's plea that the poet intercede for her with her Son:

> Write a complaint
> to my Baby
> that his Mother is fading
> in the dust here
> that here there is no
> joy.

Piszi skargę / do Syneczka / że tu w kurzu mdleje Matka / tu żadne / wiesiele.

By endowing his madonnas with individual psychological quirks and allowing them to speak in a distinctive regional dialect,[17] Harasymowicz has succeeded in conjuring up from these decaying wooden figures women of flesh and blood like the real village women who once served as models for the local craftsmen. In a poem from a later collection Harasymowicz makes explicit his affection for art which takes its inspiration from humble reality. "The Czech Master Teodoryk" is dedicated to a Czech painter of religious subjects who chose to reveal in his portraits of the saints the moral and physical defects of his human models:[18]

> God appeared to Teodoryk
> In Czech fashion
> Not on the heights
> Of an iron bridge
> In a Gothic heaven
> But in a roll
> In a turnip
> In old clogs
> In a detail from the world.

Bóg objawił się Teodorykowi / Na czeski sposób / Nie na wysokościach / żelaznego mostu / Gotyckiego nieba / Ale w bulce chleba / Ale w rzepie / W starych chodakach / W detalu świata.

A similar "Czech fashion" of extracting poetry from the ordinary is one of the wellsprings of Harasymowicz's aesthetics. In this respect, too, he can be compared with Białoszewski, although stylistically the two poets are quite obviously worlds apart.

V. *Grotesques*

The gentle poetry described in the preceding sections has its striking obverse in Harasymowicz's monstrous fairy tales and coarse "hooligan" poems. *Miracles* and *Return to the Land of Gentleness* depicted a naive poet's vision of an idyllic world.

Wieża melancholii (The Tower of Melancholy, 1958), chronologically the sequel to these early volumes, is a nightmare world where sexuality and violence are grotesquely blended. The transition from the sweet innocence of the first two books to the horrors of the third is as startling as if Gauguin had moved in the course of two years from his bright primitivism to a savage surrealism. Two examples should suffice to illustrate this sea change.

In "Papal Toys" the poet fancies himself a "pope of the imagination," perched on a Pacific island throne, his feet propped on a fish painted by Salvador Dali (an unnecessary allusion to the obvious surrealism of the work). The poet-pope weaves fantasies about two naked girls seated at opposite ends of a saw, who knit red gloves for him while the saw between them slices a soldier in half. Other dismembered soldiers serve as the "pope's" water skis.[19] "Ballad with a Lily about Red-Haired Little Princesses" is a rape-murder fantasy with a rural setting: the rape is to be committed in a barnyard where the princesses will be tied with thread to pillars of frosting, after which a billy goat will butt them to death while an ax sheds tears.[20] (It remains unclear if the ax weeps because of the slaughter or in frustration at its exclusion from the bloodshed.)

In these poems, images from nature still abound, although the surrealism of the "plots" permits the introduction of sea images into Harasymowicz's normally land-locked settings. Nature in this context no longer serves Harasymowicz as a peaceful retreat from the world; it is too suffused with the savagery which the poet's fantasies generate. In the title poem of *Tower of Melancholy* the violence he has conjured up eventually destroys the poet himself. Here the natural world is depicted in grotesque metaphors. The poet-owner of the castle foresees his own death in a fire set by a frog-headed dwarf. The sea, visible from the tower of his condemned fortress, is likened to a stomach ripped open by wolves; the sun, to an eyeless, skinned head; and the trees are said to howl like madmen. The "civilized" world, too, is implicated in the mesh of violence which ensnarls both man and nature, through the use of a simile comparing the spider webs (symbols of decay) to frost-coated telephone wires.[21]

VI   *Cracow and the Merging of Past and Present*

Harasymowicz's poems on contemporary Cracow are not as feverishly violent as the surrealistic ballads of *Tower of Melancholy,* but reveal a kindred fascination with ugliness and cruelty. They can be said to stand midway between the regional landscape poetry and the surrealistic fantasies of violence, linked to both groups of poems by the poet's antiauthoritarian, antitraditionalist stance. As early as 1958, in the long poem "Cracow," Harasymowicz had explored the theme of a medieval city surviving into the vulgar contemporary age, its past glories shining through the dull surface of the present.[22]

Harasymowicz returned to the theme of Cracow as a city of contradictions in *Bar na Stawach* (The Bar at the Ponds, 1972). In this volume he developed yet another lyrical persona—one almost diametrically opposed to the "I" of the Carpathian poems. Coining a new word, "lumpen poetic," to describe himself, he poses as a cross between a bohemian and a hooligan, a poet who is attuned to the "lumpen metaphors" of city life.[23] In keeping with this new brash image, the metaphors of *Bar at the Ponds* are deliberately coarse and sometimes violent. Lower-class Cracow slang replaces the regional dialects found in the pastoral Carpathian poems. In the long, programmatic piece which closes *Bar at the Ponds,* "Central Harasymowicz Park," the "new" Harasymowicz, in wordy imitation of the lumpen poems of Warsaw poet Białoszewski, defiantly mocks poetic tradition and flaunts the free life of the poet-tramp: "the people are wiping their paws / on the white shirt front of classicism"; "the moon has become an item / of daily use"; "I whistled and pissed a silver triumphal arch / and all of Cracow lay beneath it"; "real poetry is hiding now in the daily newspapers."[24]

From our present perspective *Bar at the Ponds* appears to be an aberration. The lumpen-poet pose may simply have been an experiment, a flirtation with a new persona to which the poet may not return. What is genuine in these poems and consistent with both the earlier and later work—apart from the generous use of vivid metaphors which is Harasymowicz's signature—is the poet's revulsion against the overly materialistic society developing in Poland.

Harasymowicz's recent collection of poetry, *Barokowe czasy* (Baroque Times, 1975), returns once again to the theme of Cracow. *Baroque Times* is introduced with the epigraph, "Wawel grows inside me with every passing day." Taking Wawel Castle as a symbol of the entire span of Poland's history, the forty-five poems of *Baroque Times* combine to form a mosaic meditation on the vicissitudes of Polish history and the poet's role as interpreter and defender of the national tradition. This interest in Poland's heroic past is further developed in the 1976 volume, *Banderia prutenorum czyli Chorągwie pruskie podniesione roku pańskiego 1410* (Banderia prutenorum or Prussian Banners Raised in the Year of Our Lord 1410), which celebrates the Polish victory over the Prussians in the battle of Grunwald. A curious collection of some fifty brief poems, each describes a specific banner captured by the Poles, as illustrated by one Stanisław Durinka in the year 1448. Harasymowicz has become so absorbed in the glorification of Poland's past that recently he has even changed his name to a hyphenated form, Harasymowicz-Broniuszyc, which has a hoarier ring to it.

Yet even in *Baroque Times,* with its explicit affirmation of the poet's role as defender in verse of the glorious deeds of ancestral Poles and Ukrainians,[25] Harasymowicz is drawn to baroque Cracow as much for aesthetic as for ideological reasons:[26]

> When
> I approach this place
> as a pilgrim of verse
>
> There is
> the ceaseless joy
> of whitewashed
> perspectives.

Kiedy / podchodzę tu / pielgrzymką wierszy / / Jest nieustanna radość / bielonych wapnem / perspektyw.

VII *Astride a Wooden Table*

The dominant theme in Harasymowicz's recent poetry, to which two books and numerous individual poems in other collections are devoted, is the subject of poetry itself. (A subtheme of this is the poet's role in the world he creates out of words and his obligation to that world.) *Zielnik, czyli wiersze dla wszystkich* (An Herbarium, or Verses for Everyone, 1972) and *Żaglowiec i inne wiersze* (Sailboat and Other Poems, 1974) are composed for the most part of tiny haikulike poems—a significant change from Harasymowicz's usual loosely structured, rambling poems compounded of many brief stanzas. Most of these miniatures are reflections on the poet's art or the nature of his inspiration, deliberately couched in homely images:[27]

> Unmindful of holidays
> imagination daily
> roams like a bear
> the black honey of verse
> spurts from the beech trees
>
> Unmindful of holidays
> the ursine hunger
> for word-berries within me. . . .

Bez względu na święta / wyobraźnia codziennie / jak niedźwiedź wędruje / z buczyn wyciska / czarny wierszy miód / / Bez względu na święta / słów-jagód we mnie / niedźwiedzi głód. . . .

Harasymowicz portrays himself as under some inner compulsion to write: "I reach for the word as for bread."[28] Inspiration is an external force to which the poet is obedient:[29]

> One sits at the table
> the pen stands like a nag
> no command will move her
>
> Suddenly,
> for no rhyme or reason
> feeling gallops like a flame
> along the slope of the poem
> as autumn gallops
> along a mountainside
>
> The pen breaks into a gallop
> worlds fly past

    page after page[30]
    rattles past

    I can only hold on
    to my cap
    so as not to fall
    from the table

Siedzi się przy stole / pióro stoi jak szkapa / żaden jej rozkaz nie niesie / / Nagle / ni stąd ni zowąd / uczucie pędzi jak płomień / poematu zboczem / jak górskim zboczem / pędzi jesień / / Pióro rzuca się w cwał / przelatują światy / turkoczą / stroną za stroną / / Ja przytrzymuję tylko / czapkę / żeby nie spaść / ze stołu.

This rather simplistic dramatization of poetic inspiration, with its deliberate avoidance of the notion that poets labor at their craft, employs a number of Harasymowicz's favorite devices. The downgrading of myths, noted above in connection with religious motifs, appears here in the metamorphosis of Pegasus, a traditional symbol of poetry, into a broken-down nag which is further domesticated into a wooden table. The fleeting references to autumn and mountain slopes are shorthand allusions to the autumnal Carpathian landscapes which Harasymowicz's faithful readers will recognize as his special environment. The lines are brief, broken into independent phrases; though the poem looks "modern" in typography, the lack of punctuation and capitalization neither complicates the reading of the poem nor enhances it by allowing for ambiguity. Basically this is a straightforward, quite simple poem, as are the great majority of Harasymowicz's verses despite their contemporary dress.

As a rule, Harasymowicz's world in his poems on poetry is circumscribed by his kitchen in which his table, Pegasus, stands and his teakettle sings; his universe is encompassed by his house and garden. His verbal magic alone gives this world life:[31]

    Wherever my wounded
    verse
    passes
    blood can be found
    all over the leaves.

Gdzie przejdzie / mój ranny / wiersz / wszędzie na liściach / zostawia krew.

(The word "ranny" means both "wounded" and "early." Because of this dual meaning, the bloody traces left by the poems represent both the birth pains of creation and the reflected light of a crimson sunrise—injury and healthy awakening simultaneously.)

Harasymowicz's preoccupation with the theme of his own poetry appears to be an indirect confession that he is not, after all, really confident that his creative powers are as great as he claims. In "Primer" the poet mocks his art, reversing his usual terms of comparison and revealing the ordinary objects behind his typical imagery: a real house hides behind the image of a sleeping ox with smoke wafting from its ears; a credenza has been mistaken for a fat-bellied bishop; a sack of grass is really only a man.[32] The larger world is reduced once more to the dimensions of a single household.

The dangers of self-delusion about one's gifts are explored in the cycle "Sunday."[33] In a mood of self-doubt the poet voices the suspicion that he has attempted to usurp the Creator's privileges and then defends himself by insisting that his books are a testament of faith. He declares that it would be blasphemous to rival God as a creator. His duty as a poet made by God is to let words evoke already created reality. Finally, Harasymowicz arrives at a temporary and not very satisfactory resolution of the issue with the declaration that the poet serves God with his pen:[34]

> Words no longer believe in miracles
>
> . . . .
>
> However on the mountain of this table
> my hand miraculously multiplies words
> and much has come forth from it in praise of the Lord.

Słowa już nie wierzą w cuda / / . . . / / Jednak na tej górze stołu / moja ręka cudownie mnoży słowa / i wielu wyszło stąd chwaląc Pana.

The long poem "The Sailboat" continues this wrestling with religious faith in a more impassioned manner. The poet, "a fat fellow with a sick heart and an excess of imagination," claims he has been seeking God all his life through his poetry and yet he remains "in the pagan woods of my own fantasies / where the hooting of irony like the hooting of owls / echoes through the night."[35]

It can be expected that this unresolved theme will reappear in Harasymowicz's future writings.

VIII *Conclusion*

Jerzy Harasymowicz has remained aloof from and hostile to contemporary Polish society, picturing himself variously as a celebrant of unspoiled nature in an increasingly industrialized world, as a connoisseur of undervalued folk art, as a bohemian hanger-on of the urban lumpen proletariat (instead of the preferred proletarian class), and a master sorceror who possesses the verbal wizardry to replace the real world with one of his own conjuring. Alternately hostile and expansive, he ranges in his poetry from naive expressions of wonder at the miracle of a bullfinch's being to bizarre fantasies of murder and torture—always in a world which he controls.

His poetic output is of uneven quality and of widely disparate thematic concerns. It is marked by formal simplicity and a striving for effect by the accumulation of inventive metaphors and striking visual imagery. The world of poetry has become Harasymowicz's private retreat, encompassing the antagonistic realms of his adopted region whose natural landscape and waning folk culture he evokes so imaginatively; the nightmare world of his surrealistic fantasies in which he remains the controlling power; the idealized historical past and the deviant present. In his recent work even his created world has not seemed private enough, and he has retreated a step beyond it to a solipsistic preoccupation with his own imagination. His faith in his poet's power to create his own world has diminished; his self-doubt, which emerges as a form of religious searching has, perhaps, opened new perspectives on his twenty-year poetic career.

CHAPTER 10

Stanisław Grochowiak:
In Defense of the Ugly

THE name Stanisław Grochowiak is linked with the word
"turpizm"—a literary label coined by Polish critics to denote the antiaesthetic of the ugly which erupted onto the literary
scene in the years of the Thaw. "Turpizm" (from the Latin
"turpis"—"vile," "base," "ugly") provides a witty anagrammatic
pun in Polish, converting neatly into "trupizm" (corpse-ism)—
an apt term for Grochowiak's fascination with death and bodily
decay.[1] Both these obsessions—with physical decomposition and
with the aesthetically unsavory—converge in Grochowiak's treatment of sexuality, which is divorced in his poetry from sentiment
and spirituality.

Grochowiak's deliberate emphasis on the ugly, his emphatic
rejection of transcendence, was aimed in part against the buoyant
optimism represented by Julian Przyboś. When Przyboś in turn
lashed out against the "Generation of '56" in his intemperate "Ode
to the Turpists" (1962), Grochowiak was one of his prime targets.[2]
Przyboś thundered forth his disgust at the "turpists'" muse, which
he dubbed "Pegasus-the-Rat," and expressed disdain for their
fascination with a Parnassus turned into a garbage dump reeking
of rats and excrement, and for their vision of man as a skeleton.
In the swirling controversies that surrounded the new ugliness
in art the vituperative rhetoric of Przyboś's poem could pass as
a contribution to the debate over poetry's proper direction. From
our present perspective, however, it is clear that Przyboś's reaction was exaggerated almost to the point of hysteria and that
it overlooked in relation to Grochowiak, at least, one of the most

154

striking aspects of this "turpist's" art. For all his preoccupation with offensive subject matter and shockingly crude images, Grochowiak never rejected the values of poetic form or cultural tradition. His poetry is far more traditional in its structure than are the works of such nonconformist poets as Tadeusz Różewicz and Miron Białoszewski.

I *Biographical Note*

Stanisław Grochowiak was born in 1934 in the industrial town of Leszno in what was then the extreme western region of Poland. His childhood was disrupted, of course, by the Nazi occupation, but the many references in his poetry to the horrors of the extermination camps reflect a voluntary concern with the moral issues which were for older survivors an inescapable burden imposed by experience. Grochowiak received his high school and university education in Communist Poland, studying Polish literature at the universities of Poznań and Wrocław. He entered adulthood as the first harbingers of the post-Stalinist Thaw made their appearance in Poland. His debut as a poet coincided with the debuts of Herbert, Białoszewski, and Harasymowicz. Unlike these poets, Grochowiak did not adopt the stance of an outsider alienated from the literary profession. He began by working for the state-approved Catholic publishing house, Pax. From 1958 through 1960 he was associated with the Warsaw literary journal, *Współczesność* (The Contemporary), which served briefly as an organ of the "Generation of '56." During the 1960s and 1970s he served on the editorial boards of a number of other literary journals, including *Nowa Kultura* (New Culture), *Kultura* (Culture), and *Poezja* (Poetry).

Grochowiak's first volume of poetry, *Ballada rycerska* (Knight's Ballad) was published in 1956. That same year saw the publication of his novel *Plebania z magnoliami* (The Presbytery with Magnolias). A prolific writer, over the next twenty years he published ten more volumes of prose (including short stories, novels, and plays), a number of works for children, and an anthology of Polish poetry. Grochowiak died in Warsaw in 1976 at the age of forty-two.

II *Death and Desire*

Knight's Ballad already displayed almost the entire range of
strengths and weaknesses of Grochowiak's poetic *oeuvre*. His
characteristic themes—death, the sexual drive, the triumph of
commonplace vulgarity, and the unique integrity of art—are all
present. Many of the images are stunning in their harshness, but
many others lose their effect through their too obvious intention
to shock. The poems reveal Grochowiak's interest in the use
of traditional forms of prosody to express contemporary concerns.
The best are striking statements of Grochowiak's solemn view of
the spiritual darkness in which mankind endures. The worst
are merely offensive or demonstrate a foolish sentimentality.
These are also the extremes of Grochowiak's later poetry.

Knight's Ballad opens with "A Prayer" in which the first two
lines provide an immediate antidote to any thoughts of spiritual
uplift the title may have engendered.[3] In his apostrophe to the
Virgin as "Mother of God of the Angels / Mother of God of the
Spiders" ("Matko Boska od Aniołów / Matko Boska od pają-
ków"), Grochowiak pronounces his central thesis which can be
traced throughout his poetry: whatever spiritual aspirations man
may have, he is forever mired in his animal nature. The very
choice of the spider—the Dostoevskian symbol of dread—is significant, for there is something in Grochowiak's grim vision of a
lust-ridden humanity which seems to reveal the Russian writer's
imprint.

Grochowiak's earliest work, like some of his late poetry, is
relatively mellow. (The full-blown concentration on the vile
which earned him the name of "turpist" dates from his second
volume of poetry, *Menuet z pogrzebaczem* [Minuet with a Poker,
1958].) But even at its mellowest, Grochowiak's poetry is marked
by a strange blend of sentimentality and unfeeling caricature,
of lyric impulses with elements of the grotesque. Such an admixture has its Polish roots in the Skamander movement of the
1920s, particularly in the verse of Julian Tuwim, and in the
further development of this tendency in the poetry of Konstanty
Ildefons Gałczyński. Both these poets were drawn to depictions
of the vulgarity of petty bourgeois life, which they claimed to
despise but from which they seemed incapable of averting their

scornful attention. "The Widower," a poem from *Knight's Ballad*, clearly demonstrates Grochowiak's mocking distortion of the lyric impulse by the introduction of grotesque detail:[4]

> I took your bridal veil
> I wrapped it in a crumpled newspaper—
> And that was as brutal
> As pain.
>
> Then your delicate slippers,
> Those sweetest, dearest little boats of yours,
> And I put your earrings, two drops of dew,
> Into an empty Maggi box.
>
> At night I rattle that box,
> I weep over the package with your veil,
> In my grief I burrow into my chair
> Which is empty
> Cold
> No good.
>
> I still have the soap you left,
> With which you soaped your breasts,
> Soaped your steaming hair,
> And soaped your nose—even your nose.
>
> I kiss this slippery pebble,
> I devour this slippery pebble—
> There's not enough left for tomorrow,
> My God, that's when hunger begins.

Wziąłem twój ślubny welon, / W pomiętą zwinąłem gazetę— / I było takie brutalne / Jak ból. / / A potem pantofle najczulsze, / Łódeczki najmilsze, najdroższe, / I w puszce od maggi schowałem kolczyki, / Dwie krople rosy. / / Nocą podzwaniam tą puszką, / Płaczę nad paczką z welonem, / Kopię w rozpaczy w krzesło / Puste, / Zimne, / Niedobre. / / Mam jeszcze mydło po tobie, / Którym mydliłaś piersi— / Włosy mydliłaś gorące, / I nos mydliłaś—i nos. / / Całuję ten śliski kamyczek, / Pożeram ten śliski kamyczek— / Na jutro mi już nie wystarczy, / Mój Boże, i zacznie się głód.

Characteristically ·Grochowiak focuses his depiction of the widower's grief on the physical apprehension of loss. His wife's

death has destroyed the cozy domesticity which is revealed in
his references to her slippers, his armchair, and the now empty
box of soup flavoring. The widower's attachment to the piece of
soap, whose disintegration is as inevitable as that of the woman's
body it once caressed, is bizarre but utterly convincing. The
poem is a miniature psychological portrait which anticipates the
grotesque narratives of the late 1960s.

   In a sense, the erotic poetry of *Minuet with a Poker* and the
next volumes, *Rozbieranie do snu* (Undressing for Sleep, 1959)
and *Agresty* (Gooseberries, 1963), demonstrates an effective
safeguard against the kind of psychological disintegration which
"the widower" experiences. The male personae of Grochowiak's
blatantly "turpist" poems rarely choose a recognizable, whole
woman as the object of their desires. The female described in
the title poem of *Undressing for Sleep*, for example, is a ghoulish
incarnation of a muse, whose purpose is to lead the poet to his
death. She is described as "dressed in pitch black" garments,
"with a greenish bald spot." She is "deaf in both black stars"
and "blind in both sharp ears." The poet stands meekly beside
her like a decapitated John the Baptist.[5]

   An untitled poem from the same collection, using the metaphor
of musical performance for the sexual act, opens with the following dehumanizing fantasy of the desired female:[6]

> When she is placed on notes it is easier than in hay
> Bluish in her nakedness Lacking a face
> I dream of a woman in red stockings
> And in gloves arranged whitely in the design

Na nutach położona lżej niżby na sianie / Niebieskawa w nagości Po-
zbawiona twarzy / Marzy mi się kobieta w czerwonych pończochach /
I rękawiczkach biało umieszczonych w planie

In "Act Amidst a Landscape" the woman is imagined as the
centerpiece in a landscape of putrefaction:[7]

> Oh be for me the mother of hanging spider webs
> Of stagnant pools in their still decaying warmth
> Be for me a madonna of landscapes fragrant
> With a sparrow half eaten by patient ants

O bądź mi matka pajęczyn wiszących / Bajorek stojących w niedo-
gniłym cieple / Bądź mi madonna pachnących pejzaży / Wróblem jed-
zonym przez cierpliwe mrówki

One of Grochowiak's most famous poems is a hymn to desire—
not exclusively sexual, but described in erotic imagery. "The
Breasts of the Queen are Turned Out of Wood" is a paean to the
life-force and idealism of the young, and a savage denunciation
of the hideously distorted world which is impervious, and even,
perhaps, fatal, to such vitality:[8]

> The hands of the queen are smeared with grease
> The ears of the queen are plugged with cotton
> In the mouth of the queen gypsum dentures
> The breasts of the queen are turned out of wood
>
> And I brought here a tongue warm with wine
> In my mouth rustling sparkling saliva
> The breasts of the queen are turned out of wood
>
> In the house of the queen a yellow candle withers
> In the bed of the queen a water bottle grows cooler
> The mirrors of the queen are covered with tarpaulins
> In the glass of the queen a syringe is rusting
>
> And I brought here a vigorous young belly
> Also teeth tensed like instruments
> The breasts of the queen are turned out of wood
>
> From the hair of the queen leaves are falling
> From the eyes of the queen a spider web slips down
> The heart of the queen bursts with a soft fizzle
> The breath of the queen yellows on the windowpane
>
> And I brought here a dove in a basket
> And a whole bunch of golden balloons
> From the hair of the queen leaves are falling

Ręce królowej posmarowane smalcem / Uszy królowej pozatykane
watą / W ustach królowej sztuczna szczęka z gipsu / Piersi królowej
utoczone z drewna / / A ja tu przyniosłem język ciepły winem / W

ustach szumiącą musującą ślinę / Piersi królowej utoczone z drewna / / W domu królowej więdnie żółta świeca / W łożu królowej termofor ziębnieje / Lustra królowej zakryte brezentem / W szklance królowej rdzewieje strzykawka / / A ja tu przyniosłem młody brzuch napięty / Zęby napięte niby instrumenty / Piersi królowej utoczone z drewna / / Z włosów królowej opadają liście / Z oczu królowej spada pajęczyna / Serce królowej pęka z cichym sykiem / Oddech królowej żółknieje na szybie / / A ja tu przyniosłem gołębia w koszyku / Całą wiązankę żółtych baloników / Z włosów królowej opadają liście

The outrage expressed by Grochowiak at the world being unequal to his dreams of goodness and beauty is akin to what must have been the first stage of the existential despair into which the war generation was driven by history. But Grochowiak's despair, as expressed in his poetry, is lacking a philosophical foundation; his rage has no historically determined target. Grochowiak's enemy is death, but unlike Przyboś who shared a similar obsession, he does not battle against mortality by revelling in life. Rather, he cedes the victory to death from the first.

An important feature of Grochowiak's poetry is his use of erotic imagery to represent this obsessive concern with death. "The Breasts of the Queen" is basically a metaphor for the inevitable confrontation beween idealistic dreams and the harsh crudeness of reality; but, typically, Grochowiak portrays this conflict as the thwarting of a vigorous young man's sexual desire by the loathsome body of a woman on the brink of death, whose physical decrepitude is described in repulsive detail. Grochowiak's lyric hero is always acutely aware of death when he is contemplating a woman as a sexual partner. Death is the constant guardian of the lovers' bed. In an untitled poem from *Gooseberries* the paradoxical parallel between the needs of the dead and those of the living is so persuasively pursued that in the end the marriage bed merges with the grave:[9]

> For lovers the same effort as for the dead,
> Just six boards are needed,
> The same amount of dimmed light.
>
> For lovers the same services as for the dead,
> Surround the room of love with fear,
> Don't let the children in.

For lovers, mournful in their joy, the same garments
Before the door is slammed shut.
Before earth is scattered
The heaviest brocade will fall from their bodies.

Dla zakochanych to samo staranie—co dla umarłych, / Desek potrzeba
zaledwie też sześć, / Ta sama ilość przyćmionego światła. / / Dla
zakochanych te same zasługi—co dla umarłych, / Pokój z miłością
otoczcie bojaźnią, / Dzieciom zabrońcie przystępu. / / Dla zakochanych—posępnych w radości—te same suknie, / Nim drzwi zatrzasną. /
Nim zasypią ziemię, / Najcięższy brokat odpadnie z ich ciał.

The intertwined love / death theme with, in some poems, references to the body as putrefying flesh, is not, of course, Grochowiak's invention. Baudelaire is an obvious modern precursor, and
his influence, or at least a suggestive parallel, can be detected
in Grochowiak's portrayal of sexuality and in his deliberate use
of metaphors based on human physiology to depoeticize external
reality. In the poem "For lovers," however, Grochowiak is following a far older literary tradition. The structure of this poem,
based on a pattern of implied antitheses which merge through
their very opposition, is derived from the baroque, as is the
love-as-death theme. Such imitation of baroque structures and
moods appears frequently in Grochowiak's poetry of the early
1960s.

In "When Nothing Remains Any Longer" the speaker idealizes
his erotic fantasies as a means of saving the woman from death,
comparing this to Rembrandt's attempts to lend immortality to his
beloved wife, Saskia:[10]

Some day I shall seat you naked amidst opulence
There will be garments there heavy as water
Stockings fragrant with apples

There will be broad headdresses
And metal

I want to have you naked in a dark landscape
Dense with bronzes chandeliers vases
From which the steam of vanilla punch should rise
Into the flaring nostrils of motionless dobermans

Rembrandt felt this need when he painted Saskia
Receding constantly into her own death
As if he wanted to restrain her by the weight of the grapes
To overwhelm her with the light of precious chandeliers

Kiedyś usadzę cię nagą wśród przepychu / Będą tam suknie ciężkie
jak woda / Będą pończochy o zapachu jabłek / Będą na głowę na-
krycia szerokie / I będzie metal / / Chcę mieć cię nagą w krajobrazie
ciemnym / Gęstym od brązów świeczników waz / Z których niech
dymi waniliowy poncz / W rozdęte chrapy nieruchomych dogów / /
Czuł tę potrzebę Rembrandt kiedy Saskię / Malował coraz w śmierć
swą odchodzącą / Jak by chciał wstrzymać ją wagą winogron / Przy-
gnieść świeczników drogocennych światłem

The visual richness of this poem is one of Grochowiak's most
characteristic devices. While not referring to any one canvas by
Rembrandt, it alludes both to the many portraits of Saskia in
which she is almost weighed down by her rich attire and to the
sensual nude canvas of the Danaë. Grochowiak often shapes his
poems as if he were himself painting or contemplating a canvas.
He pays attention to spatial arrangements, perspective, color, and
texture. Some of the poems are so visually explicit as to engage
the reader not only in the usual act of interpretation but in the
mental creation of a canvas as well. Others are descriptions of
specific paintings or contain references to the style of particular
artists. There are casual references to Bruegel, Bosch, Gauguin,
Renoir, and Picasso, among others, in poems which are not cen-
trally concerned with these artists. Among the poems devoted to
specific artists are "Utrillo or the origin of color," "Anatomy lesson (Rembrandt)," "Bruegel (II)," and "Bellini's Pieta.'"[11]
More than one critic has commented on Grochowiak's affinity with
the Flemish school of painters. Grochowiak was particularly attracted to Bruegel, whose colorful canvases of village and small
town folk, with their attention to grotesque detail, is echoed in
the poet's portrayal of scenes from ordinary Polish life.

III Faith Destroyed

Although Grochowiak's penchant for the grotesque and the
disgusting and his preoccupation with death do not appear to

be a direct legacy of his wartime experience, the memory of the war dead is a haunting minor theme in his works. One of his finest poems is a perfect blend of his peculiar grotesque vision with the theme of the unending repetitive horror of human history, a subject familiar to us in its entirely different presentation by poets such as Miłosz and Szymborska.

In "A Christmas Carol" Grochowiak employs the traditional Polish carol form (*kolęda*) to offer a modern revision of the miracle at Bethlehem. The *kolęda* traditionally celebrates the journey of the magi and the miracles attending the birth in the manger. Grochowiak uses these thematic features as well as traditional form (rhymed stanzas composed of four lines of eleven syllables each). But, his shepherd and wise men are figures from the nightmare world of the Nazi occupation, and the Savior remains unborn because his Mother is a victim of torture. The religious promise of salvation and the secular notion of historical progress are both savagely denied:[12]

> They converge slowly—one might almost say they're crawling—
> Some splashed with oil to the whites of their eyes,
> Others with large crooked thumbs,
> All of them riddled with holes like ruins or sculptures.
>
> The old women. . . . Shrouded in dough to their elbows;
> The widows. . . . Powdered as if by a snowstorm;
> The maidens. . . . So thin one can see their skeletons;
> The girls for hire. . . . After three nights of abstention.
>
> Representing the beasts are a goat, two rooks, a camel—
> (The camel's from the Zoo, his lip is pierced),
> An ostrich decked out in a faded cockade,
> A raven tied up in a cataract-blindfold.
>
> The kings bring up the rear. One sports a gas-mask snout.
> The second king's jaws are sealed with plaster.
> The third is blond, he's almost handsome
> In his sharp crown of iron splinters.
>
> And they stand there. Looking. The Mother
> Hangs strung between two trees. Her feet are dangling,

A drop occasionally shatters the dead silence,
At times a mouse squeaks or a stone bursts into song.

And the fetus—How long can the body be tortured?
How long can a star fall in our bowels?
At times a mouse squeaks, at times a rock bursts into song,
But that is all that has happened till now. . . .

Schodzą powoli—tak złażą się, rzekłbyś— / Jedni oliwą po białka schla-
pani, / Inni z wielkimi krzywymi kciukami, / Wszyscy dziurawi jak
gruzy lub rzeźby. / / Baby. . . . Te w ciasto spowite po łokcie; /
Wdowy. . . . Te w pudrze jak w śnieżnej zamieci; / Panny. . . . Tak
chude, że świeci szkielecik; / Płatne panienki—po trzynocnym poście.
/ / Ze zwierząt koza, dwa gawrony, wielbłąd— / (Wielbłąd ze ZOO,
ma przekłutą wargę, / Szpic ustrojony w spłowiałą kokardę, / Kruk—
jak w przepaskę—owinięty w bielmo. / / Króle na końcu. Król w gazo-
wym pysku, / Drugi ma gipsem zlutowane szczęki, / Trzeci jest jasny,
jest nieomal piękny / W ostrej koronie z żelaznych odprysków. / / I
stoją. Patrzą. Matka między drzewa / Rozpięta—zwisa. Stopy się
kołyszą. / Czasami kropla wstrząśnie martwą ciszą, / Czasem mysz
ćwierknie lub kamień zaśpiewa. / / A płód—Jak długo może drążyć
ciało? / Jak długo gwiazda spada w naszych trzewiach? / Czasem mysz
ćwierknie, czasem głaz zaśpiewa, / A to jest wszystko, co dotąd się
stało. . . .

IV Away from "Turpizm"

The profound pessimism of "A Christmas Carol" and of the
vast majority of Grochowiak's work from the first decade of his
poetic career is tempered in the verse from the second decade
by a shifting of attention to other people's lives and by a readiness
to experiment with a wider range of themes and styles. These
changes appear to have been related to the poet's more intimate
acquaintance with mortality through his father's death in the
early 1960s and his own serious illness. Throughout this period,
Grochowiak's eye remained alert to grotesque details, to be
sure, but the viciousness of the earlier period had been subdued,
and his grotesque effects were more often funny than horrifying.

In the last decade of his life Grochowiak experimented with
a number of different poetic styles and topics. One of these was
the anecdotal narrative poem devoted to bizarre events in the

lives of ordinary people. "Short Story (I)," for example, begins as a low-key meditation on an abandoned garden which once was the setting for tea parties given for her three old friends by a certain general's widow. The elegiac mood prompted by the narrator's early observations is overturned by his description of the fates of the elderly women. Not only has the general's widow had her foot severed by a trolley car (this we were told at the outset), but rumor has it that one of the other ladies died by swallowing an embroidery needle, another was accidentally strangled in church by her own rosary, while the whereabouts of the fourth lady are unknown.[13]

"Short Story (I)" was originally published in the collection *Nie było lata* (There Was No Summer, 1969); Grochowiak reprinted it in *Bilard* (Billiards, 1975) as part of an eight-poem cycle bearing the decidedly eccentric title "Delikatne umieranie periferii" ("Refined Dying in the City's Outskirts"). This cycle includes such deliberately pointless anecdotes as the one about a plucky woman who survived a trolley car crash while en route to Warsaw to sell her home-slaughtered veal.[14] The gist of another poem can be gathered from its title, which is "He Wanted to Murder His Mother with a Hammer but a Bulldozer Gobbled Him Up."[15] In both these works, as in others, the influence of Białoszewski is apparent, particularly in "He Wanted to Murder His Mother," where the narrator speaks a substandard Polish studded with urban slang. Grochowiak's poems, however, are no match for the linguistic inventiveness that characterizes Białoszewski's "little narratives."

In his last years Grochowiak appears to have been seeking a new voice. He tried out a number of styles in addition to his experimental imitations of Białoszewski. In 1969, the year *There Was No Summer* appeared, he also published a curious little book called *Totentanz in Polen* (Dance of Death in Poland).[16] It consists of a selection of sketches by a German artist, Wilhelm Petersen, who participated in the Nazi drive through Poland in September, 1939, and later published his sketches and journal under the title which Grochowiak borrowed for his book. The sketches are printed on the upper left pages of *Totentanz*; beneath them Grochowiak has placed translated excerpts from Petersen's journal. On the right-hand pages are poems by Gro-

chowiak which are meant to unmask the vileness of the Nazi
Petersen and yet show that the artist in him responded, despite
his ideology, to the suffering humanity in Poland. Unfortunately,
Grochowiak's verse is bombastic and, if anything, undermines
the poignancy of the clash between Petersen's callow words and
his moving sketches.

Billiards contains several new departures for Grochowiak.
Among them is the cycle "The Polish Year," composed primarily
of poems evoking characteristic Polish moods or scenes appropriate to the different months of the calendar. Their novelty
lies in a certain eighteenth-century archness of composition.
Billiards concludes with a cycle called "Attempts at Epic," the
showpiece of which is an ambitious tribute to Chile's assassi-
nated president Salvador Allende.

Grochowiak's last volume of poetry, the posthumous *Haiku-
images*, consists of 105 haikulike poems (three lines each, around
a central image). The range of these "haiku" is wide: some simply
provide a concise vehicle for Grochowiak's macabre fear of
death, some present evocative images from nature, and others
are attempts at philosophical witticisms. A small sampling of
these poems should give a sense of the range of this last work:

Vengefulness[17]
The foxes devour the chickens of my fear
I surrounded myself with a palisade
With bladders of drums—on one of them is the skin of
my face

Lisy pożerają kurczęta mojego lęku / Otoczyłem się palisadą / Pęcherz-
ami bębnów—na jednym z nich jest skóra mojej twarzy

Chimneys[18]
They are the children of smoke
Not its parents
Just as a lung is born from a sigh of agony

Są dziećmi dymu / Nie jego rodzicielami / Tak jak płuco się rodzi z
westchnienia agonii

Zen (5)[19]
Zen—oh lamp in which the moth is caught

It flutters about but I have no hands
Only my large swollen eyelids move slowly

Zen—lampo w której uwiązł motyl nocy / Trzepoce się a ja bez rąk /
Jedynie wielkie obrzmiałe powieki poruszają się wolno

Skylark[20]
When a child is born—no one believes in death
When a house is built—who thinks about ruins
A fish swims in its stream as merrily as a skylark

Kiedy dziecko się rodzi—nikt nie wierzy w śmierć / Kiedy dom budują
—kto wspomni o ruinie / Ryba płynie tak figlarnie w potoku jakby
była skowronkiem

V *Conclusion*

Like Różewicz and Białoszewski, Grochowiak rejected inherited concepts of "the beautiful" and "the poetic." Like Szymborska
and Herbert, he had no quarrel with accepted poetic forms.
Indeed, his poetry is not at all experimental in its structure.
Grochowiak's fame (or notoriety) stems from his use of unex-
ceptionable formal devices to express what was, in the late
1950s and early 1960s, Polish poetry's most outrageously nihilistic
vision.

The shock value of this *enfant terrible's* imagery began to
wear thin with the passage of time, and Grochowiak was seeking
in the years before his untimely death for new themes and a
new poetic vehicle for his thoughts. His experiments pointed in
several directions, but their disparate styles only served to under-
line the unifying thread in Grochowiak's work. Whether writing
"haiku" or imitations of Zen parables, disquisitions on revolutionary heroes or anecdotal descriptions of ordinary men, Grochowiak's mind was continually obsessed with the thought of
death. It appears likely that his "meandering personality" (in
Miłosz's apt phrase)[21] together with his morbid obsession, would
have condemned him to an endless circling around the major
themes of death and desire which have been described in this
chapter.

CHAPTER 11

Afterword

IN discussing the literary careers of the ten major poets presented in the preceding chapters great emphasis was placed
on Poland's political history, because its reflection in the lives
and works of Polish poets is what sets Polish poetry apart—in this
century as in the last. Although English poets, too, have at times
allowed political concerns to occupy a central place in their
writings (among twentieth-century poets, W. H. Auden and
Stephen Spender are prominent examples), political-historical
consciousness has never been central to the English poetic tradition.

Such a focus on the unique features of the Polish tradition,
however, carries the risk of obscuring the common ties with
other literatures. As suggested in the text, the poets studied
here have not been indifferent to Western literary traditions, or
to other poets' quests for solutions to aesthetic and substantive
problems. For example, Miłosz, Herbert, Szymborska, and
Grochowiak cherish and exploit in their poetry the literary and
artistic traditions which were the common heritage of all Western
literatures. Even the rejection of poetic traditions as in Różewicz
and Białoszewski is not unique to Polish literature but has ana-
logues elsewhere, most notably in postwar German poetry, where
similar moral and aesthetic reactions were at work.

The meditative, discursive tendency in Polish poetry, represented here by Miłosz and Herbert, has roots in English literature which extend past Auden to Eliot and as far back as John
Donne. The preoccupation with objects as ultimately more
reliable and more knowable than abstract concepts—an important
feature in the works of Białoszewski, Różewicz, Herbert and
Szymborska—is also a feature of contemporary American poetry,
particularly in the work of William Carlos Williams and younger

168

poets under his influence. Disdain for the traditionally beautiful, combined with a celebration of the commonplace and/or the ugly from the perspective of a disaffected outsider, as seen in the poetry of Białoszewski, Grochowiak, and to a certain extent, Harasymowicz and Różewicz, is somewhat analogous to the poetic rebellion of the American beat generation.

Such parallels are meant to be suggestive rather than exact. Broad areas exist in which contemporary Polish poetry might fruitfully be compared with American and English poetry among others, but such a comparative perspective is beyond the scope of this book.

Notes and References

Chapter Two

1. For an excellent study of the various movements in the Polish avant-garde see Andrzej Lam, *Polska awangarda poetycka* (Cracow: Wydawnictwo Literackie, 1969).

2. Jerzy Kwiatkowski, *Świat poetycki Juliana Przybosia* (Warsaw: PIW, 1972) offers a perceptive and persuasive interpretation of the evolutions of Przyboś's themes and motifs.

3. In *Utwory poetyckie* (Warsaw: Ludowa Spółdzielnia Wydawnicza, 1975), a retrospective collection prepared by Przyboś but published posthumously, the poet significantly relegated most of the poems from *Śruby* and *Oburącz* to the last third of the book. Unless otherwise indicated, all page references to Przyboś's work in subsequent notes will refer to this volume. Original volume titles will be noted in parentheses.

4. "Dachy" (*Śruby*, 1925), pp. 397–98.

5. "Dynamo" (*Śruby*), p. 400.

6. "Centrum" (*Oburącz*, 1926), pp. 416–17.

7. "List" (*Równanie serca*, 1938), pp. 57–58.

8. "Jadłospis" (*Sponad*, 1930), p. 429.

9. For a contrasting case, see the discussion of Czesław Miłosz and catastrophism in chapter 2. The most extreme prophet of social and political apocalypse was the playwright and novelist, Stanisław Ignacy Witkiewicz (1885–1939).

10. *Równanie serca* (Equation of the Heart, 1938), p. 54.

11. "U szczytu drogi" (*Póki my żyjemy*, 1944), p. 129.

12. "Wiosna 1941," "Wiosna 1942" (*Póki my żyjemy*), pp. 135, 143.

13. "Jesień 42" (*Póki my żyjemy*), p. 148.

14. "List do brata na wieś," dated April 4, 1953 (*Najmniej słów*, 1955), pp. 216–17.

15. "Nowy Kraków," dated May, 1953 (*Najmniej słów*), p. 215.

16. "Wiosna 1956" (*Narzędzie ze światła*, 1958), pp. 261–62.

17. "Gmachy" (*Sponad*), p. 436.

18. "Chaty" (*W głąb las*, 1932), p. 53.

19. "Drogą" (*W głąb las*), p. 48.

20. "Od ubiegłego roku," dated 1938, (*Miejsce na ziemi*, 1945), p. 108.

21. "Notre-Dame" (*Równanie serca*), p. 90; "Przed Notre-Dame po latach" (*Narzędzie ze światła*), pp. 268–69; "Notre-Dame III" (*Kwiat nieznany*, 1968), pp. 375–76.

22. "Ów halcyon" (*Na znak*, 1965), p. 13.

23. This key phrase also echoes the opening word of the passage, "dziw," and the closing word of the first line, "prawdziwie"—literally, "truly," from the root *-praw-*, but phonetically composed of *pra-* ("arch-," "proto-") and *dziw*.

24. "Żyjąc" (*Miejsce na ziemi*), pp. 106–7.

25. "Wstęp do poetyki" (*Więcej o manifest*, 1962), pp. 557–58.

26. "Świat się oddala," (*Próba całości*, 1961), pp. 510–13.

27. "Chowanka" (*Na znak*), pp. 590–91.

28. "Wiersz staroroczny" (*Więcej o manifest*), pp. 319–20.

29. "Mostar" (*Kwiat nieznany*), pp. 360–61.

30. "Wiosna 1969," pp. 386–87. (This poem was not published in a separate verse collection.)

Chapter Three

1. In *Native Realm: A Search for Self-Definition*, trans. Catherine S. Leach (Garden City: Doubleday, 1969), p. 248. Polish original: *Rodzinna Europa* (Paris: Instytut Literacki, 1959).

2. *Dolina Issy* (Paris: Instytut Literacki, 1955).

3. Miłosz has written an essay on Oscar V. de L. Milosz, "Bronisława Ostrowska and *Miguel Mañara*," in *For Wiktor Weintraub: Essays in Polish Literature, Language and History*, ed. Victor Erlich et al. (The Hague: Mouton, 1975), pp. 293–306.

4. See his essay "Nie," *Kultura* (Paris), no. 5/43 (1951), pp. 3–13, for his first published explanation of the decision to go into exile.

5. Miłosz's works which are available in English include: *Bells in Winter*, trans. Miłosz and Lillian Vallee (New York: Ecco Press, 1978); *Emperor of the Earth: Modes of Eccentric Vision* (Berkeley: University of California Press, 1977); *Selected Poems*, trans. Miłosz et al. (New York: Seabury, 1973); *Polish Postwar Poetry: An Anthology* (Harmondsworth: Penguin, 1970); *The History of Polish Literature* (New York: Macmillan, 1969); *The Captive Mind*, trans. Jane Zielonko (New York: Knopf, 1953).

6. "Do księdza Ch." (*Trzy zimy*, 1936), in Czesław Miłosz, *Utwory poetyckie: Poems* (Ann Arbor: Michigan Slavic Publications, 1976), pp. 6–7. Unless otherwise indicated all page references in the

notes to this chapter will refer to *Utwory poetyckie*. The original volume of publication will be noted in parentheses.

7. "Kraina poezji" (*Ocalenie*, 1945), pp. 71–73. The word "kraina" is usually associated with a mythical or fairy land.

8. "Biedny poeta" (*Ocalenie*), p. 98; "The Poor Poet," trans. Miłosz, in *Selected Poems*, pp. 53–54.

9. "Biedny chrześcijanin patrzy na getto" (*Ocalenie*), pp. 100–1; "A Poor Christian Looks at the Ghetto," trans. Miłosz, in *Selected Poems*, pp. 49–50.

10. "Piosenka o końcu świata," (*Ocalenie*), p. 95; "A Song on the End of the World," trans. A. M., in *Selected Poems*, p. 57.

11. "W Warszawie" (*Ocalenie*), pp. 115–16.

12. "Traktat moralny" (*Światło dzienne*, 1953), pp. 143–56.

13. "Toast" (*Światło dzienne*), in Czesław Miłosz, *Wiersze* (London: Oficyna Poetów i Malarzy, 1967), pp. 183–200. It is worth noting that this exceedingly biting work has been omitted from the 1977 *Utwory poetyckie* by, it can be assumed, a more mellow and forgiving author.

14. "Dziecię Europy" (*Światło dzienne*), pp. 122–26; "Child of Europe," trans. Jan Darowski, in *Selected Poems*, pp. 59–64.

15. See n. 5. This subject is also prominent in such poems as "Poeta," "Toast," "Na śmierć Tadeusza Borowskiego" (all from *Światło dzienne*) and the lengthy *Traktat poetycki* (Paris: Instytut Literacki, 1957) where it forms part of a larger investigation of the roots of contemporary Polish poetry. *Traktat poetycki* is Miłosz's clearest assessment of the various movements in Polish poetry since the turn of the century and of his own place in the history of contemporary poetry. The poem is so specific in its references as to be virtually inaccessible to readers who are not already acquainted with twentieth-century Polish literature. Because of its obscurity for the general reader, *A Treatise on Poetry* will not be discussed here; interested readers are referred to the work itself or to Miłosz's *The History of Polish Literature* for a drier, academic evaluation of the period.

16. Miłosz has published six new volumes of poetry in emigration: *Światło dzienne* (1953), *Traktat poetycki* (1957), *Król Popiel i inne wiersze* (1962), *Gucio zaczarowany* (1965), *Miasto bez imienia* (1969), *Gdzie wschodzi słońce i kędy zapada* (1974). All were published by the Paris firm, Instytut Literacki.

17. "Sposób" (*Miasto bez imienia*), p. 319.

18. For a searching critical appreciation of Miłosz's poetry from the 1930s see Kazimierz Wyka, "Ogrody lunatyczne i ogrody pasterskie" (1946) in *Rzecz wyobraźni*, 2d ed. (Warsaw: PIW, 1977), pp. 265–90.

19. "To Raja Rao," in *Selected Poems*, pp. 29–31.

20. "Rzeki maleją" (*Gucio zaczarowany*), p. 260; "Rivers Grow Small," trans. Miłosz, in *Selected Poems*, p. 28.

21. From "Po ziemi naszej" (*Król Popiel i inne wiersze*), pp. 241–47; "Throughout Our Lands," trans. Miłosz and Peter Dale Scott, in *Selected Poems*, pp. 81–88.

22. "Rok" (*Miasto bez imienia*), p. 275; "The Year," trans. Miłosz and Richard Lourie, in *Selected Poems*, p. 116.

23. "Dar" (*Gdzie wschodzi słońce i kędy zapada*), p. 350; "The Gift," trans. Miłosz, in *Selected Poems*, p. 117.

24. See note 22.

25. "Rady" (*Miasto bez imienia*), p. 313; "Counsels," trans. Miłosz, in *Selected Poems*, pp. 109–10.

26. "Czesław Miłosz: A Poet's Road to Ithaca Between Worlds, Wars, and Poetics," *Books Abroad* 43 (1969):17–24.

27. "O aniołach" (*Gdzie wschodzi słońce i kędy zapada*), pp. 347–48; "On Angels," trans. Miłosz, in *Selected Poems*, p. 111.

Chapter Four

1. For further biographical details see Lesław M. Bartelski's introduction to Tadeusz Gajcy, *Utwory wybrane: Wiersze—Poematy—Proza* (Cracow: Wydawnictwo Literackie, 1968), pp. 5–29.

2. See Wyka's famous contemporary critique, "List do Jana Bugaja," reprinted in his *Rzecz wyobraźni*, 2d ed. (Warsaw: PIW, 1977), pp. 58–71.

3. The major sources on Baczyński's life and work are Kazimierz Wyka, *Krzysztof Kamil Baczyński (1921–1944)* (Cracow: Wydawnictwo Literackie, 1961) and Zbigniew Wasilewski, ed., *Żołnierz poeta czasu kurz . . . : Wspomnienia o Krzysztofie Kamilu Baczyńskim* (Cracow: Wydawnictwo Literackie, 1967).

4. "Widma," *Utwory wybrane*, pp. 144–60.

5. "Misterium niedzielne," ibid., pp. 161–213.

6. "Do potomnego," ibid., pp. 214–20.

7. "Biała magia," *Utwory zebrane* (Cracow: Wydawnictwo Literackie, 1979), 1:244–45.

8. "Dwie miłości," ibid., 2:47–48.

9. "Szklany ptak: Poemat—baśń," ibid., 1:199–211.

10. There have been several studies of "key words" in Baczyński's poetry, but none has yet examined the semantic fields in which the frequent references to glass and other transparent material appear. Among the more interesting studies on this aspect of Baczyński's art are: Jerzy Kwiatkowski, "Potop i posąg," in *Klucze do wyobraźni:*

Szkice o poetach współczesnych (Warsaw: PIW, 1964), pp. 7–30; Ireneusz Opacki, "Elegia optymistyczna: O poezji Krzysztofa Baczyńskiego," *Roczniki Humanistyczne*, 15, no. 1 (1967):145–77; Aleksandra Okopień-Sławińska, "Semantyka poetycka a metoda jej opisu: Na przykładzie poezji Baczyńskiego," *Roczniki Humanistyczne*, 19, no. 1 (1971):299–306.

11. This theme appears in various guises, with differing interpretations, in the works of such major writers as Jerzy Andrzejewski, Tadeusz Borowski, Czesław Miłosz, and Tadeusz Różewicz.

12. "Modlitwa II," *Utwory zebrane* 1:361.

13. "Oddycha miasto ciemne długimi wiekami," ibid., 2:33–34.

14. "Rodzicom," ibid., 2:62–63.

15. "Wybór," ibid., 2:70–74.

16. See, for example, "Dalmacja" and "Madrygał," ibid., 2:428–29; 1:87.

17. "Piosenka," ibid., 1:91–92.

18. "Wesele poety," ibid., 1:260–67.

Chapter Five

1. For English translations of the plays see: Tadeusz Różewicz, *The Card Index and Other Plays*, trans. Adam Czerniawski (New York: Grove Press, 1970) and "Birth Rate: The Biography of a Play for the Theatre," in *Twentieth-Century Polish Avant-Garde Drama: Plays, Scenarios, Critical Documents*, ed. and trans. Daniel Gerould (Ithaca: Cornell University Press, 1977), pp. 269–79. A broad sample of Różewicz's poetry is available in English translation: Tadeusz Różewicz, *Selected Poems*, trans. Adam Czerniawski (Harmondsworth: Penguin, 1976) and Tadeusz Różewicz, *"The Survivor" and Other Poems*, trans. Magnus J. Krynski and Robert A. Maguire (Princeton: Princeton University Press, 1976).

2. Robert Jay Lifton discusses some typical attributes of "survivor complex" in "On Survivors," in *History and Human Survival* (New York: Random House, 1970), chap. 2.

3. "Lament" (*Niepokój*), in Tadeusz Różewicz, *Poezje zebrane*, 2d ed. (Wrocław: Ossolineum, 1976), pp. 9–10. Unless otherwise indicated all page references refer to this volume.

4. Tadeusz Borowski (1922–1951) began as a poet but is best known for his concentration camp stories, *Pożegnanie z Marią*, collected in English under the title *This Way for the Gas, Ladies and Gentlemen*, trans. Barbara Vedder (Harmondsworth: Penguin, 1976).

5. See note 3.

6. "Ocalony" (*Niepokój*), p. 19.

7. See for example "Maska," p. 7, and "Rachunek," p. 51, both from *Niepokój*.

8. "Kasztan" (*Czerwona rękawiczka*, 1948), p. 62.

9. "Powrót" (*Czerwona rękawiczka*), p. 65.

10. See for example "Ballada o karabinie" (*Uśmiechy*, 1955), p. 135; "Yenderan" (*Wiersze i obrazy*, 1952), pp. 184–87; "Wiosenny siew na Korei" (*Wiersze i obrazy*), p. 199.

11. "Czas który idzie" (*Czas który idzie*, 1951), p. 178.

12. "Zostawcie nas" (*Poemat otwarty*, 1956), p. 327.

13. "W środku życia" (*Poemat otwarty*), pp. 331–32.

14. See "Drzewo" (*Srebrny kłos*, 1955), p. 244.

15. "Formy" (*Formy*, 1958), p. 336.

16. "Zdjęcie ciężaru" (*Zielona róża*, 1961), p. 456.

17. See for example "Rozebrany" (*Formy*), p. 347, and "Karmienie Pegazu" (*Nic w płaszczu Prospera*, 1963), p. 510.

18. "Żart patetyczny" (*Rozmowa z księciem*, 1960), p. 403.

19. "Rozmowa z księciem" (*Rozmowa z księciem*), pp. 386–89.

20. "Przygotowanie do wieczoru autorskiego," *Proza* (Wrocław: Ossolineum, 1973), pp. 575–86.

21. "Rachunek" (*Niepokój*), p. 51.

22. "Drobne ogłoszenia liryczne" (*Rozmowa z księciem*), p. 412.

23. "Szybciej niż w marzeniu" (*Czas który idzie*), p. 169; "Dytyramb na cześć teściowej" (*Uśmiechy*), pp. 110–11.

24. "Róża" (*Niepokój*), p. 7.

25. See note 15.

26. "Z dziennika żołnierza" (*Głos anonima*, 1961), pp. 499–506; "Białe groszki" (*Rozmowa z księciem*), p. 401.

27. "Świat 1906–Collage," pp. 470–73 and "Fragmenty z dwudziestolecia," pp. 474–75, both from *Zielona róża*.

28. "Wśród wielu zajęć" (*Twarz trzecia*), p. 575.

29. "Et in arcadia ego" (*Głos anonima*), pp. 480–98; "Spadanie" (*Twarz trzecia*), pp. 592–99; "Non-Stop-Shows" (*Twarz trzecia*), pp. 606–13.

30. For an excellent analysis of this poem and of Różewicz's yearning for a return to innocence, see Ryszard Przybylski, *Et in arcadia ego: Esej o tęsknotach poetów* (Warsaw: Czytelnik, 1966), chap. 3.

31. English translation by Krynski and Maguire, p. 119.

32. Ibid., p. 131.

33. Ibid., p. 135.

34. Ibid., p. 143.

Chapter Six

1. For an account of the circumstances surrounding the original publication of these poems and a description of the works which have not yet been reissued, see Adam Włodek, "Debiut z przygodami," *Miesięcznik Literacki* 3, no. 10 (1968):44–50.

2. "Stara robotnica," *Wiersze wybrane* (Warsaw: PIW, 1964), pp. 12–13.

3. "Pieśń o zbrodniarzu wojennym," ibid., pp. 14–15.

4. "Z Korei," ibid., p. 16.

5. "Rehabilitacja," *Poezje* (Warsaw: PIW, 1970), pp. 34–35.

6. These volumes are: *Wołanie do Yeti* (Warsaw: Wydawnictwo Literackie, 1957); *Sól* (Warsaw: PIW, 1962); *Sto pociech* (Warsaw: PIW, 1967); *Wszelki wypadek* (Warsaw: Czytelnik, 1972); *Wielka liczba* (Warsaw: Czytelnik, 1976); *Wiersze wybrane* (see note 2); *Poezje* (see note 5).

7. "Z nie odbytej wyprawy w Himalaje," *Poezje*, pp. 44–45.

8. "Dwie małpy Bruegla," ibid., p. 38.

9. Except for the first line which contains only twelve syllables, all the long lines of the poem are composed of thirteen syllables with a caesura (or pause) after the seventh syllable. This is a standard line in traditional Polish prosody. With the exception of one isolated seven-syllable line, the shorter lines are arranged in pairs whose total syllables add up to thirteen (in combinations of seven + six, or eight + five—both traditional resolutions of the obligatory division within a longer verse line).

10. "Cień," *Poezje*, p. 58.

11. "Buffo," ibid., pp. 48–51.

12. "Jestem za blisko," ibid., pp. 85–86.

13. "Przy winie," ibid., pp. 75–76.

14. "Powroty," *Wszelki wypadek*, p. 20.

15. "Miłość szczęśliwa," ibid., pp. 42–43.

16. "Monolog dla Kassandry," *Poezje*, pp. 118–19.

17. This poem appeared under the title "Zdziwienie" in the "new poetry" section of *Poezje* (p. 163) and, otherwise unaltered, under the title "Zdumienie," in *Wszelki wypadek* (p. 28).

18. "Wszelki wypadek," *Wszelki wypadek*, pp. 5–6.

19. "Odkrycie," ibid., pp. 21–22.

20. "Pod jedną gwiazdką" ibid., pp. 45–46.

Chapter Seven

1. *Pamiętnik z powstania warszawskiego* (Warsaw: PIW, 1970);

English translation by Madeline G. Levine, *A Memoir of the Warsaw Uprising* (Ann Arbor: Ardis, 1977).

2. *Obroty rzeczy* (Warsaw: PIW, 1956).

3. Joseph Alsop, "Boguslaw Sent Me," *The Boston Globe*, June 6, 1959. See Miron Białoszewski, *Teatr osobny, 1955–1963* (Warsaw: PIW, 1973) for a collection of scenarios and "songs" from the private theater's programs.

4. In addition to works referred to in the above notes Białoszewski has published: *Rachunek zachciankowy* (Warsaw: PIW, 1959); *Mylne wzruszenia* (Warsaw: PIW, 1961); *Było i było* (Warsaw: PIW, 1965); *Donosy rzeczywistości* (Warsaw: PIW, 1973); *Szumy, zlepy, ciągi* (Warsaw: PIW, 1976); *Wiersze* (Warsaw: PIW, 1976), a retrospective poetry collection; and *Zawał* (Warsaw: PIW, 1977).

5. See pp. 80–81 above.

6. "Szare eminencje zachwytu," (*Obroty rzeczy*); *Wiersze*, p. 43.

7. "Sprawdzone sobą," (*Rachunek zachciankowy*); *Wiersze*, p. 84.

8. In "Wiwisekcja," *Teatr osobny*, pp. 17–36 and "Wyprawy krzyżowe," ibid., pp. 81–105.

9. "rodowód góry odosobnienia," (*Mylne wzruszenia*); *Wiersze*, p. 142.

10. This is a complicated pun. "Upiekło jej się" means "she escaped," but with the unconventional addition of the subject "getto" (in Polish) to a usually impersonal expression, we also get the meaning "the ghetto burned down (for her)." See Stanisław Barańczak, *Język poetycki Mirona Białoszewskiego*, Z Dziejów Form Artystycznych w Literaturze Polskiej no. 41 (Wrocław: Ossolineum, 1974), p. 53. Barańczak also points to other linguistic peculiarities of this poem. "Karmel," for example, is given a feminine gender although it should be a masculine noun. Barańczak suggests that the gender change is occasioned by the quilt's belonging to a woman. It would apear equally possible that it becomes feminine by analogy with the feminine noun for quilt, "kołdra."

11. From "Romans z konkretem," *Rachunek zachciankowy*, pp. 29–30.

12. See Barańczak, for a thorough discussion of child-language features in Białoszewski's writings.

13. Parts 4 and 5 of "Leżenia," (*Mylne wzruszenia*); *Wiersze*, pp. 137–38.

14. "Ballada o zejściu do sklepu," (*Obroty rzeczy*); *Wiersze*, p. 76.

15. See Michał Głowiński, "Małe narracje Mirona Białoszewskiego," *Teksty*, no. 6 (1972), pp. 9–28.

16. "Ze spacernika," *Było i było*, p. 30.

17. "Opowieść Lu. He.," ibid., p. 17.

18. "Spiszę wszystko," *Szumy, zlepy, ciągi*, pp. 7–9 (italics mine).
19. "18 maja dalej," *Było i było*, p. 92.
20. The best studies of Białoszewski's language, both excellent pieces of scholarship, are Barańczak's monograph (see n. 9 above), to which I am heavily indebted in this chapter, and Stanisław Dan-Bruzda, "O 'Obrotach rzeczy' Mirona Białoszewskiego," *Pamiętnik Literacki* 52, no. 4 (1961):425–76.
21. "Hepyent (1)" (*Mylne wzruszenia*), *Wiersze*, p. 189.
22. *Pamiętnik z powstania warszawskiego*, p. 46.

Chapter Eight

1. Herbert has published the following books: *Struna światła* (Warsaw: Czytelnik, 1956); *Hermes, pies i gwiazda* (Warsaw: Czytelnik, 1957); *Studium przedmiotu* (Warsaw: Czytelnik, 1961); *Barbarzyńca w ogrodzie* (Warsaw: Czytelnik, 1962; 2d ed. 1964); *Napis* (Warsaw: Czytelnik, 1969); *Dramaty* (Warsaw: PIW, 1970); *Wiersze zebrane* (Warsaw: Czytelnik, 1971); *Pan Cogito* (Warsaw: Czytelnik, 1974).
2. "Do Apollina" (*Struna światła*), *Wiersze zebrane*, pp. 21–23. Unless otherwise noted all page references in this chapter are to this edition.
3. "Do Marka Aurelego" (*Struna światła*), pp. 29–30.
4. "Jonasz" (*Studium przedmiotu*), pp. 246–47.
5. "Brak węzła" (*Napis*), p. 326. I have borrowed the translation of the title of this piece from Zbigniew Herbert, *Selected Poems*, trans. John Carpenter and Bogdana Carpenter (New York: Oxford University Press, 1977), p. 16.
6. "Żołnierz" (*Hermes, pies i gwiazda*), p. 191.
7. "Pięciu" (*Hermes, pies i gwiazda*), pp. 128–30.
8. "Prolog" (*Napis*), pp. 291–93.
9. "Powrót prokonsula" (*Studium przedmiotu*), pp. 248–49; translation by Czesław Miłosz, in Zbigniew Herbert, *Selected Poems*, trans. Miłosz and Peter Dale Scott (Baltimore: Penguin, 1968), pp. 96–97.
10. "Tren Fortynbrasa" (*Studium przedmiotu*), pp. 250–51.
11. "Kołatka" (*Hermes, pies i gwiazda*), pp. 94–95.
12. "Stołek" (*Struna światła*), p. 60.
13. "Krzesła" (*Studium przedmiotu*), p. 285.
14. "Kura" (*Hermes, pies i gwiazda*), p. 182.
15. "Kamyk" (*Studium przedmiotu*), p. 265; translation by Czesław Miłosz, in Herbert, *Selected Poems* (1968), p. 108.
16. "Studium przedmiotu" (*Studium przedmiotu*), (1968) pp. 260–64; translation by Czesław Miłosz, in Herbert, *Selected Poems* (1968),

pp. 104–7. For two detailed and completely divergent interpretations of this work see Debra Nicholson Czestochowski, "Herbert's 'Study of the Object': A Reading," *The Polish Review* 20, no. 4 (1975):131–37, and Jarosław Marek Rymkiewicz, "Krzesło," *Twórczość* 26, no. 1 (1970):50–88.

17. "Rady," *Pan Cogito*, pp. 68–69; translation in Herbert, *Selected Poems* (1977), trans. John and Bogdana Carpenter, pp. 72–73.

18. "Potwór Pana Cogito," *Twórczość* 30, no. 7 (1974):13–15; translation in Herbert, *Selected Poems* (1977), trans. John and Bogdana Carpenter, pp. 69–71.

19. "Przesłanie Pana Cogito," *Pan Cogito*, pp. 78–79; translation in Herbert, *Selected Poems* (1977), trans. John and Bogdana Carpenter, pp. 79–80.

Chapter Nine

1. Harasymowicz's debut was greeted with enthusiasm by such eminent critics as Kazimierz Wyka and Jerzy Kwiatkowski, both of whom, like the poet, lived in Cracow. He has not gained as warm an appreciation from critics who are more closely identified with Warsaw.

2. "Miasteczko w Karpatach" (*Powrót do kraju łagodności*, 1958), in *Wybór wierszy* (Warsaw: Czytelnik, 1967), p. 27.

3. "Ten wierszyk o babciach," *Wieża melancholii* (Cracow: Wydawnictwo Literackie, 1958), pp. 13–14.

4. "Strych," *Znaki nad domem* (Warsaw: PIW, 1971), pp. 75–89.

5. "Sad, styczeń," *Wybór wierszy*, p. 13.

6. "Wiek niewinności," ibid., p. 11.

7. "Prawdziwy portret autora," ibid., p. 15.

8. The literary tradition of affectionate evocations of typical Polish landscapes, impressive only in their sentimental associations, goes back to Jan Kochanowski's sixteenth-century poems on his Czarnolas estate and to Adam Mickiewicz's tribute to the Lithuanian landscape in *Pan Tadeusz*.

9. See note 3.

10. *Znaki nad domem*, pp. 5–11.

11. "W górach niepogoda," ibid., pp. 90–100.

12. "Mit o świętym Jerzym," *Wybór wierszy*, pp. 129–30.

13. See Wiesław Paweł Szymański, "Wywiady Jerzego z Madonnami," *Poezja*, no. 1 (1970), pp. 91–93.

14. *Madonny polskie* (Warsaw: Czytelnik, 1969), pp. 33–37.

15. "Madonna z miasta z Dzieciątkiem ta bez korony," ibid., pp. 42–46.

16. "Madonna pod Barcicami," ibid., pp. 10–12.

17. The excerpts quoted here from "Madonna pod Barcicami" are riddled with dialect forms: e.g., "biedy" pronounced "bidy"; the imperative "piszi" instead of "pisz"; "wiesiele" for "zabawa," "rozrywka".

18. *Bar na Stawach*, 2d ed. (Cracow: Wydawnictwo Literackie, 1974), pp. 40–45.

19. "Papieskie igraszki," *Wybór wierszy*, pp. 41–42.

20. "Ballada z lilijką o księżniczkach rudych," ibid., pp. 49–50.

21. "Wieża melancholii," ibid., p. 51.

22. "Kraków" (*Przejęcie kopii*, 1958), ibid., pp. 69–100.

23. Harasymowicz's poses show more than a faint resemblance to the famous poet of rural Russia and bohemian Moscow, Sergej Esenin (1895–1925).

24. *Bar na stawach*, pp. 109–27.

25. See for example "Tyle nam zostało," *Barokowe czasy* (Cracow: Wydawnictwo Literackie, 1975), pp. 98–99, and "Stary portret," ibid., pp. 101–2.

26. "Barokowe czasy Bielany," ibid., pp. 88–90.

27. "Bez względu," *Zielnik, czyli wiersze dla wszystkich* (Cracow: Wydawnictwo Literackie, 1972), p. 71.

28. "Życiorys," ibid., p. 46.

29. "Narowistość pióra," ibid., p. 57.

30. This is a pun. "Strona za stroną" may be translated as either "page after page" or "region after region."

31. "Czerwień jesieni," *Żaglowiec i inne wierszy* (Warsaw: Instytut Wydawniczy Pax, 1974), p. 21.

32. "Elementarz," *Zielnik*, p. 78.

33. "Niedziela," *Żaglowiec*, pp. 84–103.

34. "Piszący stół," ibid., p. 91.

35. "Żaglowiec," ibid., pp. 104–13.

Chapter Ten

1. Jan Jósef Lipski makes this pun central to his argument in his brief essay, "Rekonesanse Grochowiaka," *Twórczość* 28, no. 12 (1972):96–98.

2. Julian Przyboś, "Oda do turpistów," *Utwory poetyckie*, pp. 567–69.

3. "Modlitwa," *Ballada rycerska* (Warsaw: Pax, 1956), pp. 5–6.

4. "Wdowiec," ibid., pp. 48–49.

5. "Rozbieranie do snu," *Rozbieranie do snu* (Warsaw: PIW, 1959), pp. 9–10.

6. Ibid., p. 35.

7. "Akt w pejzażu," ibid., p. 41.

8. "Piersi królowej utoczone z drzewa," ibid., pp. 20–21; translation by Czesław Miłosz, in *Polish Post-War Poetry* (Baltimore: Penguin, 1970), p. 144.

9. "Dla zakochanych to samo staranie–co dla umarłych. . . ," *Agresty* (Warsaw: Czytelnik, 1963), p. 18.

10. "Gdy już nic nie zostanie," *Rozbieranie do snu*, p. 40.

11. "Utrillo czyli powstanie koloru," ibid., p. 51; "Lekcja anatomii (Rembrandta)," *Agresty*, pp. 39–40; "Brueghel (II)," *Nie było lata* (Warsaw: Czytelnik, 1969), p. 57; "Bellini 'Pieta'," *Bilard* (Warsaw: Czytelnik, 1975), p. 18.

12. "Kolęda," *Agresty*, p. 41. Wiesław Paweł Szymański has published an excellent analysis of this poem, " 'Kolęda' Stanisława Grochowiaka," *Poezja*, no. 5 (1971), pp. 46–52.

13. "Nowela (I)," *Nie było lata*, pp. 50–51.

14. "Ciesielska," *Bilard*, p. 107.

15. "Chciał matkę zabić młotkiem, buldożer go zeżarł," ibid., pp. 111–12.

16. *Totentanz in Polen* (Warsaw: PIW, 1969).

17. "Mściwość," *Haiku-images* (Warsaw: PIW, 1978), p. 12.

18. "Kominy," ibid., p. 24.

19. "Zen–piąte," ibid., p. 32.

20. "Skowronek," ibid., p. 43.

21. In *Polish Post-War Poetry*, p. 139.

Selected Bibliography

PRIMARY SOURCES

Because of space limitations collected or selected editions of poetry are listed when possible; individual volumes of poetry are listed only if published after the latest retrospective edition.

1. Polish Editions

BACZYŃSKI, KRZYSZTOF KAMIL. *Utwory zebrane* (*Collected Works*). 2 vols. Cracow: Wydawnictwo Literackie, 1979.

BIAŁOSZEWSKI, MIRON. *Pamiętnik z powstania warszawskiego* (Memoir of the Warsaw Uprising). Warsaw: PIW, 1970.

————. *Wiersze* (Verse). Warsaw: PIW, 1976.

GAJCY, TADEUSZ. *Utwory wybrane: Wiersze—Poematy—Proza* (Selected Works: Verse—Narrative—Prose). Cracow: Wydawnictwo Literackie, 1968.

GROCHOWIAK, STANISŁAW. *Poezje wybrane* (Selected Poetry). Warsaw: Ludowa Spółdzielnia Wydawnicza, 1968.

————. *Wybór wierszy* (Selected Verse). Warsaw: Czytelnik, 1965.

————. *Bilard* (Billiards). Warsaw: Czytelnik, 1975.

————. *Haiku-images*. Warsaw: PIW, 1978.

————. *Nie było lata* (There Was No Summer). Warsaw: Czytelnik, 1969.

————. *Polowanie na cietrzewie* (Hunting Grouse). Warsaw: PIW, 1972.

————. *Totentanz in Polen* (Dance of Death in Poland). Warsaw, PIW, 1969.

HARASYMOWICZ, JERZY. *Banderia prutenorum czyli Chorągwie pruskie podniesione roku pańskiego 1410* (Banderia prutenorum or Prussian Banners Raised Up in the Year of Our Lord 1410). Cracow: Wydawnictwo Literackie, 1978.

————. *Bar na Stawach* (The Bar at the Ponds). Warsaw: Czytelnik, 1972.

————. *Barokowe czasy* (Baroque Times). Cracow: Wydawnictwo Literackie, 1975.

183

184 CONTEMPORARY POLISH POETRY

————————. *Poezje wybrane* (Selected Poems). Warsaw: Ludowa Spółdzielnia Wydawnicza, 1971.

————————. *Polowanie z sokołem* (Hunting with a Falcon). Cracow: Wydawnictwo Literackie, 1977.

————————. *Zielnik, czyli wiersze dla wszystkich*; *Pascha Chrysta: Poemat wielkanocny* (An Herbarium, or Verses for Everyone; Christ's Passover: An Easter Poem). Cracow: Wydawnictwo Literackie, 1972.

HERBERT, ZBIGNIEW. *Pan Cogito* (Mr. Cogito). Warsaw: Czytelnik, 1974.

————————. *Wiersze zebrane* (Collected Verse). Warsaw: Czytelnik, 1971.

MIŁOSZ, CZESŁAW. *Utwory poetyckie: Poems.* Ann Arbor: Michigan Slavic Publications, 1976.

————————. *Wiersze* (Verse). London: Oficyna Poetów i Malarzy, 1967.

PRZYBOŚ, JULIAN. *Utwory poetyckie: Zbiór* (Poetic Works: A Collection). Warsaw: Ludowa Spółdzielnia Wydawnicza, 1971.

RÓŻEWICZ, TADEUSZ. *Poezje zebrane* (Collected Poems). 2d ed. Wrocław: Ossolineum, 1976.

————————. *Duszyczka* (Little Psyche). Cracow: Wydawnictwo Literackie, 1977.

SZYMBORSKA, WISŁAWA. *Poezje* (Poems). Warsaw: PIW, 1970.

————————. *Wiersze wybrane* (Selected Verse). Warsaw: PIW, 1964.

————————. *Wielka liczba.* (Large Number). Warsaw: Czytelnik, 1976.

————————. *Wszelki wypadek* (In Any Event). Warsaw: Czytelnik, 1972.

2. English Translations

BIAŁOSZEWSKI, MIRON. *A Memoir of the Warsaw Uprising.* Edited and translated by Madeline G. Levine. Ann Arbor: Ardis, 1977.

HARASYMOWICZ, JERZY. *Genealogy of Instruments.* Translated by Catherine Leach and Seymour Mayne. Ottawa: Valley Editions, 1974.

HERBERT, ZBIGNIEW. *Selected Poems.* Translated by Czesław Miłosz and Peter Dale Scott. Baltimore: Penguin, 1968.

————————. *Selected Poems.* Translated by John Carpenter and Bogdana Carpenter. Oxford: Oxford University Press, 1977. Emphasizes Herbert's later work, particularly *Pan Cogito.*

MIŁOSZ, CZESŁAW. *Bells in Winter.* Translated by Miłosz and Lillian Vallee. New York: Ecco Press, 1978.

————————. *Selected Poems.* Translated by Miłosz et al. New York: Seabury, 1973.

RÓŻEWICZ, TADEUSZ. *Selected Poems.* Translated by Adam Czerniawski. Harmondsworth: Penguin, 1976.

————. *"The Survivor" and Other Poems.* Translated by Magnus J. Krynski and Robert A. Maguire. Princeton: Princeton University Press, 1976.

Polish Post-War Poetry. Edited and translated by Czesław Miłosz. Baltimore: Penguin, 1970. The best introduction in English to postwar Polish poetry.

SECONDARY SOURCES

1. Studies of Contemporary Polish Poetry

BARAŃCZAK, STANISŁAW. *Ironia i harmonia: Szkice o najnowszej literaturze polskiej* (Irony and Harmony: Essays on Modern Polish Literature). Warsaw: Czytelnik, 1973. Includes thoughtful essays on many of the poets surveyed in this study.

BARTELSKI, LESŁAW M. *Genealogia ocalonych: Szkice o latach 1939–1944* (Genealogy of the Saved: Essays on the Years 1939–1944). Cracow: Wydawnictwo Literackie, 1969. Literary life in occupied Poland, described by a participant.

————. *Polscy pisarze współcześni: Informator 1944–1974* (Contemporary Polish Writers: A Handbook 1944–1974). Warsaw: Wydawnictwo Artystyczne i Filmowe, 1977. Brief entries containing basic biographical and bibliographical information.

BŁOŃSKI, JAN. *Zmiana warty* (Changing of the Guard). Warsaw: PIW, 1961. Collection of essays focusing on changing literary and ethical values in the post-Stalin years.

GÖMÖRI, GEORGE. *Polish and Hungarian Poetry 1945 to 1956.* Oxford: Oxford University Press, 1966. A survey of the poetry of these two East European countries, with special attention to political context and contents.

KAJTOCH, JACEK, and SKÓRNICKI, JERZY, eds. *Debiuty poetyckie 1944–1960: wiersze, autointerpretacje, opinie krytyczne* (Poetic Debuts 1944–1960: Poems, Interpretations by the Poets, Critical Opinions). Warsaw: Iskry, 1972. Bibliographical data, a handful of representative poems and critical opinions for each of twenty-three poets. An excellent introduction to the subject.

KWIATKOWSKI, JERZY. *Klucze do wyobraźni: Szkice o poetach współczesnych* (Keys to Imagination: Essays on Contemporary Poets). Warsaw: PIW, 1964. Interpretive essays and sketches by a leading critic; investigations of central obsessions, key words.

————. *Remont pegazów: Szkice i felietony* (Remodeling of Pegasuses: Sketches and Feuilletons). Warsaw: Czytelnik, 1969. Essays and reviews of poetry from the 1960s.

MACIĄG, WŁODZIMIERZ. *Literatura Polski Ludowej, 1944–1964* (The

Literature of People's Poland, 1944–1964). Warsaw: PIW, 1973.
A standard reference work, with brief stylistic sketches and bib-
liographies of scores of Polish writers. Includes a list of recipients
of major literary awards during the two decades surveyed.
MIŁOSZ, CZESŁAW. *The History of Polish Literature*. New York: Macmillan, 1969. Although published over a decade ago, still the best
and most up-to-date textbook in English.
WYKA, KAZIMIERZ. *Rzecz wyobraźni* (Product of the Imagination). 2d
ed. Warsaw: PIW, 1977. Includes penetrating essays on contemporary poets by the late dean of Polish critics.

2. Studies of Individual Authors

BARAŃCZAK, STANISŁAW. *Język poetycki Mirona Białoszewskiego.*
(Miron Białoszewski's Poetic Language.) Wrocław: Ossolineum,
1974. A meticulous analysis of Białoszewski's linguistic experi-
ments.
BŁOŃSKI, JAN. "Tradycja, ironia, i głębsze znaczenie" ("Tradition,
Irony, and Deeper Meaning"). *Poezja* (Poetry) 6, no. 3 (1970):
24–38. A thoughtful essay on Herbert's relation to literary traditions and history.
GŁOWIŃSKI, MICHAŁ. "Małe narracje Mirona Białoszewskiego" ("Miron
Białoszewski's Little Narratives"). *Teksty* (Texts), no. 6 (1972),
pp. 9–28. A study of the anecdotal prose narratives of Białoszewski.
————. "Przyboś: najwięcej słów" ("Przyboś: The More Words the
Better"). *Teksty* (Texts), no. 9 (1975), pp. 39–52. A revisionist
interpretation of Przyboś's style as wordy rather than laconic.
KOZANECKI, MARIAN. "Estetyka brzydoty w liryce Stanisława Grocho-
wiaka" ("The Aesthetics of the Ugly in Stanisław Grochowiak's
Lyric Poetry"). *Studia Estetyczne* (Studies in Aesthetics) 10
(1973):135–45.
KWIATKOWSKI, JERZY. *Świat poetycki Juliana Przybosia.* Warsaw: PIW,
1972. A fine monographic study of Przyboś's poetic vision.
LAM, ANDRZEJ. "Dialogowość poezji Herberta" ("The Dialogic Nature
of Herbert's Poetry"). *Teksty* (Texts), no. 1 (1976), pp. 86–104.
Argues that in many of Herbert's poems there are two opposing
voices.
LAPIŃSKI, ŹDZISŁAW. *O kategoriach percepcyjnych w poezji Juliana
Przybosia* (On Perceptual Categories in Julian Przyboś's Poetry).
In Studia z teorii i historii poezji (Studies in the Theory and History of Poetry), ser. 2. Wrocław: Ossolineum, 1967. A rigorous
approach to categorizing the types of perception in Przyboś's
poetry.

OPACKI, IRENEUSZ. "Elegia optymistyczna: O poezji Krzysztofa Baczyńskiego" ("An Optimistic Elegy: On the Poetry of Krzysztof Baczyński"). *Roczniki Humanistyczne* (Humanities Annals) 15 no. 1 (1967):145–77. Sees key to Baczyński's poetic vision in concept of transformation or transcendence.

PIESZCZACHOWICZ, JAN. " 'W baśni stronie': O poezji Jerzego Harasymowicza" (" 'In the Realm of the Fairytale': On the Poetry of Jerzy Harasymowicz"). *Poezja* (Poetry), no. 5 (1970), pp. 51–61. On Harasymowicz's primitivism; a polemic with Jan Prokop's interpretation.

PROKOP, JAN. "Harasymowicz–albo człowiek pierwotny" ("Harasymowicz or Primitive Man"). In *Lekcja rzeczy* (The Reading of Literature). Cracow: Wydawnictwo Literackie, 1972. Pp. 93–103. Sees Harasymowicz's primitivism as a form of escapism.

——————. "Wisława Szymborska albo wstydliwość uczuć" ("Wisława Szymborska or Emotional Shyness"). In *Lekcja rzeczy* (The Reading of Literature). Cracow: Wydawnictwo Literackie, 1972. Pp. 176–85. An analysis of the existentialist concerns behind Szymborska's poetry.

PRZYBYLSKI, RYSZARD. *Et in arcadia ego: Esej o tęsknotach poetów* (And I Too Was in Arcady: An Essay on the Yearnings of Poets). Warsaw: Czytelnik, 1966. Pp. 127–64. A masterful description of Różewicz's longing for a lost world of innocence.

SANDAUER, ARTUR. "Na przykład Szymborska" ("Szymborska for Example"). In *Liryka i logika* (Lyric Poetry and Logic). Warsaw: PIW, 1969. Pp. 391–420. Argues that the essential feature of Szymborska's poetry is the constant interweaving of reality and imagination by a keen intellect.

——————. "Poezja rupieci" ("Poetry of Junk"). In *Liryka i logika* (Lyric Poetry and Logic). Warsaw: PIW, 1969. Pp. 259–94. On the function of the ugly in Białoszewski's poetry.

——————. *Przyboś*. Warsaw: Agencja Autorska i Dom Książki, 1970. A brief study of Przyboś's poetry.

SZYMAŃSKI, WIESŁAW PAWEŁ. " 'Podwojony sam sobie jestem': O poezji Tadeusza Gajcego" (" 'I am Divided Against Myself': On the Poetry of Tadeusz Gajcy"). *Roczniki Humanistyczne* (Humanities Annals) 19, no. 1 (1971):229–39. Argues that Gajcy's work shows a fundamental struggle between dream and reality, past and present.

TRZNADEL, JACEK. "Poeta w ziemi obiecanej?" ("A Poet in the Promised Land?"). In *Róże trzecie:Szkice o poezji współczesnej* (Third Roses: Essays on Contemporary Poetry). Warsaw: PIW, 1966.

188 CONTEMPORARY POLISH POETRY

Pp. 176–85. On the echoes of medieval art and philosophy in Grochowiak's poetry.

————. "W baśni i gdzie indziej" ("In the Fairy Tale and Elsewhere"). In *Róże trzecie: Szkice o poezji współczesnej* (Third Roses: Essays on Contemporary Poetry). Warsaw: PIW, 1966. Pp. 146–75. On Harasymowicz's fantasy worlds.

VOGLER, HENRYK. *Tadeusz Różewicz.* Warsaw: PIW, 1971. The first book-length study of Różewicz.

WASILEWSKI, ZBIGNIEW, ed. *Żołnierz poeta czasu kurz . . . : Wspomnienia o Krzysztofie Kamilu Baczyńskim* (Soldier Poet the Dust of Time . . . : Recollections of Krzysztof Kamil Baczyński). Cracow: Wydawnictwo Literackie, 1967. Essays of widely varying quality and interest, but an invaluable source.

World Literature Today 52, no. 3 (1978). The entire issue is devoted to Czesław Miłosz; contains a number of fine essays by American and Polish critics.

WYKA, KAZIMIERZ. *Krzysztof Baczyński (1921–1944).* Cracow: Wydawnictwo Literackie, 1961. Still the most thorough study of the poet.

————. "O poezji Jerzego Harasymowicza" ("On Jerzy Harasymowicz's Poetry"). In *Zielnik, czyli wiersze dla wszystkich* (An Herbarium or Verses for Everyone), by Jerzy Harasymowicz. Cracow: Wydawnictwo Literackie, 1972. Pp. 5–31. In introducing *Zielnik,* Wyka focuses on the regionalism and fairy-tale imagination of Harasymowicz's earlier works.

————. *Różewicz parokrotnie* (Różewicz Several Times Over). Warsaw: PIW, 1977. A posthumous edition, including some separately published essays on Różewicz and the unfinished manuscript of a book-length study of Różewicz's art in all of of its generic manifestations.

Index